OECD INSIGHTS

From Aid to Development

The Global Fight against Poverty

Brian Keeley

This work is published on the responsibility of the Secretary-General of the OECD. The opinions expressed and arguments employed herein do not necessarily reflect the official views of the Organisation or of the governments of its member countries.

This document and any map included herein are without prejudice to the status of or sovereignty over any territory, to the delimitation of international frontiers and boundaries and to the name of any territory, city or area.

Please cite this publication as:
OECD (2012), *From Aid to Development: The Global Fight against Poverty*, OECD Insights, OECD Publishing.
http://dx.doi.org/10.1787/9789264123571-en

ISBN 978-92-64-11152-3 (print)
ISBN 978-92-64-12357-1 (PDF)

Series: *OECD Insights*
ISSN 1993-6745 (print)
ISSN 1993-6753 (online)

The statistical data for Israel are supplied by and under the responsibility of the relevant Israeli authorities. The use of such data by the OECD is without prejudice to the status of the Golan Heights, East Jerusalem and Israeli settlements in the West Bank under the terms of international law.

All websites and data were accessed in April 2012 unless otherwise noted.

Corrigenda to OECD publications may be found on line at:
www.oecd.org/publishing/corrigenda.
Revised version, June 2012
© OECD 2012

You can copy, download or print OECD content for your own use, and you can include excerpts from OECD publications, databases and multimedia products in your own documents, presentations, blogs, websites and teaching materials, provided that suitable acknowledgement of OECD as source and copyright owner is given. All requests for public or commercial use and translation rights should be submitted to rights@oecd.org. Requests for permission to photocopy portions of this material for public or commercial use shall be addressed directly to the Copyright Clearance Center (CCC) at info@copyright.com or the Centre français d'exploitation du droit de copie (CFC) at contact@cfcopies.com.

Foreword

Development has been at the core of the OECD's mandate from the very beginning; it's what the "D" in our name stands for. The drive to reduce poverty, support and improve development perspectives and create better policies for better lives has been a consistent theme of the Organisation's work for over half a century.

There have been some notable successes, and across the world millions of people have been lifted out of poverty. However, today we are faced with a new reality. The global economic landscape has changed beyond recognition since the OECD was established. Half a century ago, the focus was on co-ordinating aid efforts by the world's wealthiest countries to help people in the world's poorest regions. But since then, the global development landscape has been shaped by some key trends:

- **The world's centre of economic gravity is changing**, and developing and emerging economies are among the key drivers of global economic growth. Their dynamism is also leading to historical shifts in global governance, as reflected in the emergence of the G20 as the premier forum for global policy co-ordination.

- **There is a growing diversity of growth and development models**, which underscores the fact that there is no one-size-fits-all solution and ultimately the people who know best what a country needs to break the pernicious cycle of poverty and deprivation are the people in that country itself.

- **The nature of development financing is changing**. Many developing economies are becoming important actors in international finance, trade, investment and development co-operation. However, it remains critical that the Least Developed Countries continue to benefit from effective, predictable and sustainable development financing.

▸ **The geography and nature of poverty are changing** with a growing proportion of the world's poor living in middle-income countries and urban areas. At the same time, inequality is increasing in advanced and developing countries alike, potentially undermining further growth, social cohesion and development.

▸ **Development challenges are global challenges.** In a highly interconnected world, issues such as climate change, natural resource scarcity, and food and energy insecurity have implications for all, and call for collective and co-ordinated global action.

As much of the world struggles to recover from the worst economic crisis in 50 years, we are called upon to rethink our approach to the challenges of economic development. The time has come for a new approach and a renewed impetus for development, based on a real partnership between developed and developing countries.

As the international community approaches the target date for the Millennium Development Goals (MDGs) in 2015, this latest book in the OECD Insights series looks at the way development and aid have evolved, how the development landscape is changing, and how a new era of development partnerships can be built on the new commitments established at the Busan High-Level Forum in December 2011, and the new OECD Development Strategy.

Together we must do our utmost to reduce poverty and inequality and deliver better policies for better, more prosperous and equitable lives throughout the world.

Angel Gurría
OECD Secretary-General

Acknowledgements

The author gratefully acknowledges the advice, assistance and insights of Federico Bonaglia, Christine Graves, Raundi Halvorson-Quevedo, Sue Kendall-Bilicki, Brenda Killen, Megan Grace Kennedy-Chouane, Justin Yifu Lin, Isabel Huber, Hans Lundgren, Andrew Mold, William Nichol, Simon Scott, Janine Treves and Michael Ward.

Special thanks to J. Brian Atwood, Chair of the OECD Development Assistance Committee (DAC), and also to Patrick Love for additional research and writing.

OECD Insights is a series of primers commissioned by the OECD Public Affairs and Communications Directorate. They draw on the Organisation's research and expertise to introduce and explain some of today's most pressing social and economic issues to non-specialist readers.

Read the **OECD Insights Blog** at *http://oecdinsights.org*

Currency Note
Currency references are in US dollars unless otherwise indicated. Constant dollar values have been adjusted to account for inflation. Current dollars are the sums actually given or received.

This book has...

A service that delivers Excel® files from the printed page!

Look for the *StatLinks* at the bottom right-hand corner of the tables or graphs in this book. To download the matching Excel® spreadsheet, just type the link into your Internet browser, starting with the *http://dx.doi.org* prefix.

If you're reading the PDF e-book edition, and your PC is connected to the Internet, simply click on the link. You'll find *StatLinks* appearing in more OECD books.

CONTENTS

1. Introduction — 8
   Partners for development — 11
   Contexts: The persistence of old ideas — 13
   What this book is about — 20

2. The persistence of poverty — 22
   Why are some countries still poor? — 25
   What is the development challenge? — 33
   Special section: The Millennium Development Goals — 35

3. What is aid? — 46
   Is all aid the same? — 49
   Who provides aid? — 54
   Special section: Aid – some numbers — 60

4. Shifting development goals and motivations — 66
   Development co-operation: A brief history — 69
   What motivates aid-giving? — 77
   What are aid's objectives? — 80

5. Are we getting results? — 84
   What are the critiques of aid? — 87
   Does aid promote growth? — 89
   What does the public think? — 94
   How is success or failure measured? — 97

6. Changing relationships and policies — 102
   How can aid be made more effective? — 105
   What is the impact of corruption on development? — 113
   What is policy coherence? — 117

7. Governance matters — 124
   What is the role of governance? — 127
   What are fragile states? — 134
   How can taxation help development? — 137

8. New partners for development — 146
   How is the world shifting? — 149
   What is South-South co-operation? — 154
   By way of conclusion — 162

References — 166

1

From a young girl in Pakistan to an old farmer in Ethiopia, aid is changing people's lives. But behind these simple human stories lies the vastly complex world of development co-operation – a place filled with countless actors and numberless projects, whose aims and achievements are often misunderstood.

Introduction

1. Introduction

By way of introduction ...

In Sukkur, Pakistan, 13-year-old Hajira is standing up. She's about to answer a maths question that none of the boys in her class can manage. "She is our top student," says teacher Manzoor Ali Abbasi. Hajira's performance is impressive, but so is the fact that she's even in school. Many women and girls in Pakistan never get an education, and their literacy rates are lower than in many other parts of the region. But the Sukkur Middle School has been helped by an Asian Development Bank programme aimed at getting more children into school, especially girls. "None of the girls in this class would have gotten past grade five without the Middle School Project," says Abbasi.

In southern Ethiopia, coffee farmer Feleke Dukamo is getting a better price for his beans. "My coffee sells for nine times more than it used to," he tells the British development agency DFID. The farmer is benefiting from the Ethiopia Commodity Exchange, established in 2008 with support from the United Kingdom. Before the exchange was created, Ethiopia's 15 million smallholders had no way of knowing the market price for their coffee, so middlemen were able to buy their beans cheaply and then sell them for a big margin. The new exchange has changed that: it sends farmers regular updates on coffee prices by text messages and via a dedicated phone line, which receives 44 000 calls a day. The result is a fairer price. "Now I can aspire to a better life," says Feleke. "I've been able to buy some cattle and, as my farm grows, I can employ people to help bring in the harvest."

In Freetown, Sierra Leone, a team of doctors is just coming off its shift. They have come a long way to work here: from Hunan province in China, in fact. They will spend two years at the King Harmon Road Hospital, specialising in familiar areas like paediatrics and endocrinology, but also in more unusual disciplines for Africa like acupuncture and traditional Chinese medicine. The doctors, who are helping to maintain a formal Chinese medical presence in Africa dating back to the early 1960s, have been moved by their time here. "It's a deep experience," one of them tells the researcher Deborah Brautigam. "The people are very poor."

In Somalia, Nurse Hodan Ali is making a painful journey home. She's travelled from Canada with two doctors to spend a week in a clinic run by Islamic Relief, a non-governmental international relief and development agency. What she's seen has left the nurse feeling troubled: "It's a war zone. A lot of people are dying and a lot are on the verge of dying. It's unimaginable to put into words," she tells a reporter. "We did as much as we could but we were just a drop in the bucket, in the ocean actually."

In Paris, a panel of development economists are speaking at the OECD. Their subject is how to democratise, or open up, their field of expertise. The question has special resonance for one of the speakers, Mustapha Kamel Nabli, governor of the central bank in Tunisia, where only months earlier the people rose up and threw out the autocratic regime. His theme is governance: "Tunisia was seen as having a relatively good performance in terms of growth, but the people were not happy," he tells his audience. "Why? For me it's because they felt they were not participating in the process of decision making, they were not participating in the choices that were being made, they were not being informed adequately ..."

Partners for development

Welcome to the vast, complex and multi-faceted world of development co-operation. Its goal, in theory, is simple: to improve the lives of our planet's poorest people. Its activities and range of actors are anything but simple, and can range from one-off projects for digging village wells to multi-year global programmes targeting scourges like AIDS.

Perhaps the most familiar activity is emergency relief, the instant rescue efforts that follow disasters like the 2004 Asian tsunami or the 2010 Haiti earthquake. High profile as these may be, however, they represent but one small piece in a much bigger jigsaw. In reality, the bulk of development co-operation – whether it involves governments, non-governmental organisations (NGOs) or both – is planned out well in advance and has long-term goals, such as improving access to healthcare and education, building infrastructure, or reinforcing countries' capacity to run their own affairs. To achieve these goals, different approaches are taken, including providing grants and loans to developing countries; supplying experts, equipment and training; providing funds to the governments of developing countries directly or bypassing them altogether to build projects on the ground, and so on.

1. Introduction

The range of actors, too, is diverse. There are the donor governments, in developing and wealthy countries and – increasingly – in the new, emerging economies like China, India and Brazil, as well as in the Arab world. There are the international agencies answerable to multiple governments, like The World Bank, the United Nations, the Asian Development Bank or the OECD, which does not itself give aid but works to improve development co-operation. There are NGOs – often referred to these days as civil society organisations – like Oxfam or Doctors Without Borders. Then there are the religious charities and private foundations, like the Gates Foundation that today plays a bigger role than many governments. And, of course, there are the developing countries themselves and, within them, their own governments, agencies, NGOs... The list could go on and on.

To add even more complexity to this mix, there's the unfamiliar language spoken here – with its talk of harmonisation, fragmentation and alphabet soup of acronyms, from AfDB to ZSP. Charting a course through this maze would require a book much longer than this. But this book has a more modest purpose: it's about aid, but about more than aid. It's an attempt to look at the full spectrum of development co-operation, how it has evolved over the past 50 years, where it has failed, where it has succeeded, and the emerging trends that will help to shape where it is going.

Aid and development

In the context of driving development, this relationship is often represented as focusing around one issue – aid, or the transfer of money and resources from richer countries to poorer countries with the primary aim of alleviating misery or promoting economic and social development. Aid certainly matters: a great deal of energy is expended on measuring it, discussing it and finding ways to make it work better. It is, as we shall see, praised and condemned with great vigour. Its importance is reflected in this book, where it is discussed at some length.

But aid is just a part of development co-operation. When richer and poorer countries interact, the development prospects of the latter are shaped by far more than just what they receive in aid. Trade is a good example: it's been shown consistently that exporting is one of the most effective ways for poorer countries to become wealthier – just think of the progress of Korea, China and Mauritius, all of which have developed lucrative foreign markets. Inspired by such examples, the international community has made a major effort in recent years to support developing countries' attempts to become exporters through what is called "aid for trade", spending $100 billion between 2006 and 2009.

But, paradoxically, they have so far failed to sign off on the Doha Development Round of global trade talks, which was intended specifically to bolster the role of developing countries in global markets (*see Chapter 6*). Many developed countries also continue to financially support their own farmers, making it all but impossible for farmers in poorer countries to compete. As Brian Atwood, Chair of the OECD's Development Assistance Committee, told US legislators in 2008 (before taking up his current position), "If we … work with a country to improve its exports and its productive capacity and we deny that country access to markets, either in Europe or the United States, we're undercutting the development mission. If we … subsidize heavily our agricultural products, which we do, and we help countries to develop their own agriculture sectors, basically we're contradicting ourselves…". The bottom line: the aid and development co-operation policies of developed countries matter, but other policy areas – trade, finance, migration, taxation – are equally crucial.

Contexts: The persistence of old ideas …

Writing in the UK's *Guardian* newspaper in 2011, researcher Andrew Darnton offered a provocative take on his countrymen's attitude towards development: "In terms of perceptions of poverty, the UK public appears to be stuck in 1985." He pointed to a survey of public attitudes taken in 2009, where one respondent offered his views on how things had changed since Live Aid, the transatlantic music telethon of the mid-1980s that raised money for famine relief in Ethiopia: "What's happened since Live Aid? I was at school then. Now I'm 36 and nothing has really changed."

In fact, a huge amount has changed. Countries that were once poor are now becoming rich, and, yes, even in Africa. And thinking about aid and development co-operation has changed, and changed again. New priorities have emerged, approaches have evolved. Even the language of development co-operation has moved on.

Images linger, realities change

It's news to no one that some of the world's biggest countries have seen a huge change in their economic fortunes in recent decades. But it took the financial crisis of 2008 and subsequent recession to really highlight their new-found strength. As the traditional economic powerhouses of the OECD stuttered, emerging economies like China and India became the engines of global economic growth. What's less often realised is that these countries are not alone: among African countries, too-often collectively dismissed as an economic basket case, at least 17 non-oil economies have transformed themselves in recent decades, enjoying growth well in excess of the average in much of the developed world and laying the foundations for strong civil liberties and good governance.

In Mozambique, the economy has grown by 7.5% a year for 15 years, more than doubling average real income (although the poverty rate was stagnating at 55% in 2010 after falling from 69% in 1997). In landlocked Mali, the economy has expanded annually by 5.5% since the mid-1990s, reducing poverty by a third and allowing the completion rate in primary education to double. In Cape Verde, economic expansion has averaged 6% a year for almost two decades, a rise accompanied by a reduction in poverty rates from 40% to 20%. All these examples come from a recently published book, *Emerging Africa*, which chronicles Africa's often-overlooked economic success stories and which features a foreword by Liberia's president, the Nobel laureate Ellen Johnson Sirleaf. Her words are worth quoting at length:

> "The changes in the emerging countries since the mid-1990s are striking. Investment is growing quickly. Foreign investors that never would have thought of Africa a decade ago are lining up to look at new opportunities. Trade is expanding even more rapidly as businesses become more integrated with global markets. GDP is growing by more than 5% per year, so that average incomes in the emerging countries have increased by 50% since the mid-1990s. Political conflict has subsided, and governments are strengthening the protection of civil liberties and political freedoms. Most of the emerging countries have embraced democracy, and their ratings on

a range of governance indicators are improving. More youth are in school, from primary schools through universities, and healthcare has improved significantly. Poverty rates have been falling by one full percentage point per year for more than a decade, ushering in the most rapid decline in poverty rates ever seen on the continent. The differences between the despair and misery of the 1980s and the hope and energy of today are like night and day."

Of course, there have been transformations before, and subsequent disappointments as fresh starts turned into false dawns. Nevertheless, the mood of confidence in much of the developing world, and especially in Sub-Saharan Africa, is palpable, buoyed by increased investment and rising trade.

> "In 2002 ... Africa had just passed through a period of low growth and declining living standards that had caused widespread Afro-Pessimism. There has been a major change since then and we can now look back at a decade of African Renaissance ..."
>
> *African Economic Outlook 2011*

What has this to do with development co-operation? Simply this: the contexts for traditional forms of Western aid are evolving rapidly – **new sources of funding**, including foreign business investment, are becoming ever more important drivers of development. The role of aid, often overstated, is changing and is in some respects becoming less significant, especially in those countries that are enjoying a revival. Other flows – trade, investment, remittances (money sent home by people working abroad) – play an even greater role in determining *most* developing countries' prospects. Indeed, in most years developing countries receive three times more in such "private flows" than they do in aid from the major donor countries. Developing countries are also becoming better at raising funding for development within their own borders: in Africa, countries on average raise ten times more from taxation than they receive in aid. Another change: emerging economies like China, India and Brazil are themselves becoming both significant sources of investment and partners for development in Africa, Asia and South America.

Perceptions linger, thinking moves on

The debate over aid – does or doesn't it work? – is often sharply polarised: on one side are advocates like Jeffrey Sachs, author of *The End of Poverty* and an advisor to UN secretaries-general. Sachs is both a thinker and activist: as director of Columbia University's Earth Institute, he's a leading figure in the Millennium Villages project, an innovative approach aimed at helping Africa's rural communities to lift themselves out of poverty. Sachs believes that, as well as adopting a broad range of pro-development policies, the world's wealthiest countries should meet the long-standing target of committing 0.7% of their gross national product (GNP) to aid. On the other side of the debate is someone like Dambisa Moyo, an African-born international economist and author of the bestselling *Dead Aid*, which argues that aid creates a culture of dependency in developing countries and fuels corruption. Instead, she argues, aid flows should be sharply reduced, and eventually eliminated, forcing governments in developing countries to make greater use of other forms of financing, like taxation and foreign investment.

Unfortunately, relatively few people take the time to read the arguments of people like Sachs and Moyo directly. Most of us learn of them through over-simplified and sometimes partisan coverage in the media and on the Internet, where their arguments are often boiled down to this simple dichotomy: aid is good, aid is bad. Representing "the aid debate" in terms like these only barely reflects the reality of how aid and development co-operation are discussed by academics, governments and policy makers, and today's huge body of research and analysis. It also fails to reflect two of the great evolutions in aid thinking over the past two decades, which can now be said to form the foundations of much of today's development co-operation.

The first is the Millennium Development Goals (MDGs), a set of ambitious targets for reducing poverty and its impacts by a target date of 2015. Around the world, these goals have come increasingly to shape how development co-operation is thought of and implemented (*see special section in Chapter 2*). The second is the idea of **aid effectiveness**, which asks us to focus not on how much aid is provided but on *how* it is provided and what it achieves. This distinction is crucial: as we will repeatedly see in this book, the circumstances in developing countries – how well

1. Introduction

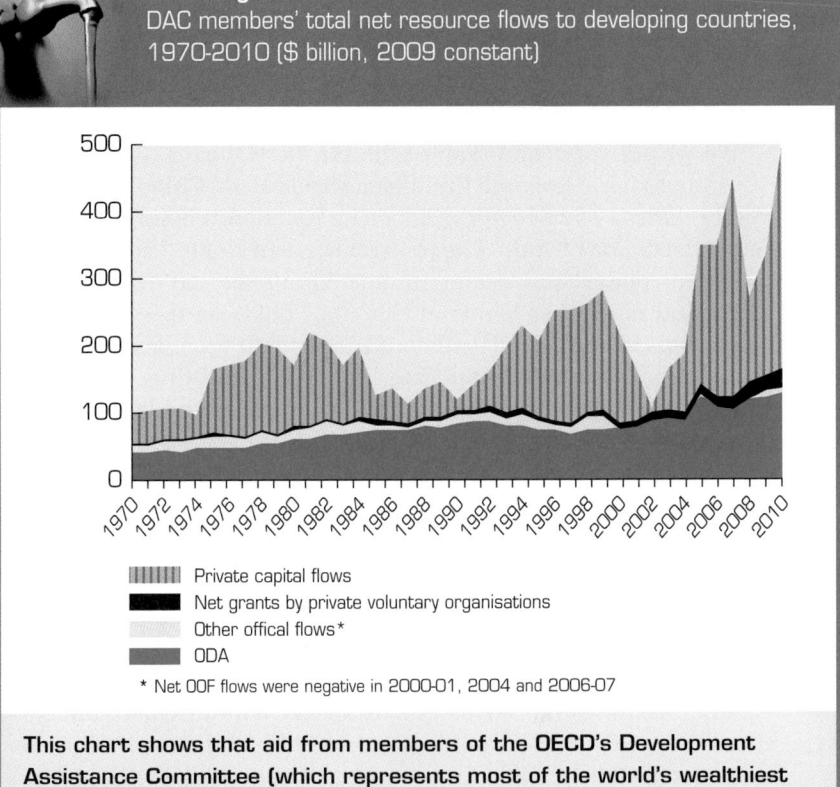

Declining share
DAC members' total net resource flows to developing countries, 1970-2010 ($ billion, 2009 constant)

- Private capital flows
- Net grants by private voluntary organisations
- Other offical flows*
- ODA

* Net OOF flows were negative in 2000-01, 2004 and 2006-07

This chart shows that aid from members of the OECD's Development Assistance Committee (which represents most of the world's wealthiest countries) is now a relatively less important source of funds for developing countries than it once was. Other private flows, such as foreign investment from businesses, have assumed a much bigger role.

Source: OECD (2011), "Detailed aid statistics: Official and private flows", *OECD International Development Statistics* (database).
StatLink ⋙ : http://dx.doi.org/10.1787/888932606169

they run their own affairs – are crucial to ensuring the success of development co-operation. Equally, the attitude of donor countries, and their willingness to let developing countries set their own agenda, has come increasingly to be seen as what makes the difference between development success and failure. A further step was taken in this direction at the High-Level Forum

OECD Insights: From Aid to Development 17

on Aid Effectiveness in Busan, Korea at the end of 2011, when governments from all parts of the development spectrum as well as civil society jointly signed up to a commitment for a new global development partnership.

Words linger, meanings evolve

"We are not very comfortable with the word 'donor'," a Chinese researcher says in Deborah Brautigam's book about China's growing role in Africa, *The Dragon's Gift*. "The recipient's hand is always below the donor's hand." The researcher is not alone: "Not only are the terms 'donor' and 'recipient' anachronistic," says the British writer and researcher Jonathan Glennie, "but even the word 'aid' itself needs to be shelved – all countries benefit from development co-operation, so a word implying charity is misleading." Glennie is, of course, right, and in recent years, much of the language of development co-operation has changed to reflect views such as his. Such a shift is welcome, and it reflects a realisation that when our poorest neighbours on this planet can improve their lives, we all benefit. To speak of "aid" in such a context, as Glennie points out, seems odd, to say the least.

And yet ... while this shift in language is welcome, it has added a new challenge to discussions of development. As a former chair of the Development Assistance Committee, Eckhard Deutscher, has noted, "Technocratic 'development speak' fails to communicate effectively and relate to political and public audiences." That is no understatement. Take, for example, the terminology that came to be used in the mid-2000s to refer to donors and recipients – "development partners" and "partner countries". Which is which? Unless you're involved in development yourself, you will probably only be able to hazard a guess. For that reason, and with some regret, this book makes use of terminology that many will regard as outdated and some as offensive. Nevertheless, terms like "aid", "recipient" and "donor" are clear and – above all – short. Where such terms are not appropriate – where, for example we are really talking about much broader development co-operation and not just aid – the text will attempt to distinguish between the two.

1. Introduction

DEVELOPMENT – THE "D" IN OECD

Development co-operation and dialogue have been at the heart of the OECD's mission since it was founded in 1961. The OECD's Development Assistance Committee (DAC), which brings together donor governments and multilateral organisations, was one of the first OECD bodies to meet. The OECD Development Centre was created soon after as a place where developed and developing nations could "meet to study in common the problems of economic development". Other entities followed, including the Sahel and West Africa Club Secretariat and the African Partnership Forum Support Unit.

On official development assistance (ODA), the OECD acts as a watchdog, monitoring aid figures and urging donor countries to live up to their commitments. The DAC monitors the development assistance performances of its members through peer reviews in which all members are able to comment on each other's policies. Over the years, the DAC has pursued a wide range of initiatives to make aid work better, including campaigning against "tied aid" and for more effective aid. Today, the OECD continues to work with developing countries, particularly fragile states, on supporting and strengthening their institutions, ensuring that they can make the most of trade opportunities, identifying ways to strengthen public services and infrastructure, and strengthening their tax administrations to mobilise additional sources of finance for development. On gender issues, initiatives like the Development Centre's SIGI Index have helped highlight how legal and social institutions prevent women from playing a full social and economic role.

The world economy has been transformed over the first 50 years of the OECD's existence, with the rapid economic emergence of countries like China and India. These developments have contributed to a renewed focus on South-South co-operation and underline the importance of increased inclusiveness in development co-operation. In 2010, these changes were reflected in the creation of the Seoul Development Consensus, which committed G20 countries "to work in partnership with other developing countries… to help them build the capacity to achieve and maximize their growth potential". The G20 recognised the long experience of the OECD, asking it to help in the creation of that consensus and to take part in its implementation. In that spirit, the OECD is creating a new, broad development strategy, with aims that include enhancing policy coherence for development and strengthening global partnerships to encourage mutual learning.

Source: Based on *Better Policies for Better Lives – The OECD at 50 and Beyond*.

What this book is about ...

Development has always been a priority for the OECD – it's the "D" in OECD *(see box on page 19)*. Although the OECD is not itself an aid agency, its member countries provide the vast bulk of the world's development assistance and the Organisation is an important player in monitoring financial commitments and in helping to shape global thinking on development co-operation. This book draws on work from the OECD to offer a brief introduction to development co-operation. To give as full a sense as possible of this work, the book includes graphics and charts from a number of OECD publications and papers as well as direct quotations from their texts. At the end of each chapter, there's a section offering pointers to further information and reading from the OECD, as well as links to other intergovernmental bodies and information sources on aid and development co-operation.

Chapter 2 examines the wider development context for development co-operation. Why do some countries thrive while others languish? Examining this question can provide useful clues on the challenges that development co-operation needs to address and on the causes and many facets of poverty. It includes a special section on the Millennium Development Goals (MDGs), which have given concrete expression to the aims of development.

Chapter 3 explores the vast and intricate world of aid and development co-operation, and who provides and receives aid, introducing many of the key actors and terms.

Chapter 4 looks at how aid and development co-operation have evolved since the 1960s, and examines the motivations and objectives of developed countries in working with their developing partners.

Chapter 5 asks about the success of development co-operation. "Does aid work?" is one of the most frequently encountered questions in development co-operation today. This chapter argues that it does, but it needs the right conditions.

Chapter 6 looks at the changing relationships within the world of development co-operation. It introduces the aid-effectiveness agenda, including the Paris Declaration on Aid Effectiveness, discusses how corruption is being tackled, and considers how policy coherence can help foster a more development-friendly environment.

Chapter 7 examines one of the key issues in development today – governance. It looks at how donors seek to address human rights through development co-operation; their increasing interest in supporting fragile states; and the role of tax in strengthening the links between citizens and states and in providing much-needed state revenues.

Finally, **Chapter 8** looks at the impact of some of the "new" partners for development – China, India, Brazil and others. As the chapter explains, many of these are not new players at all. Nevertheless, their impact is growing and helping to reshape the development landscape.

2

In a world undergoing an enormous shift in wealth, why are some countries still poor? The question might seem obvious, but the answers are not. Investigating the causes and many facets of poverty is essential to understanding the challenge for development co-operation.

The persistence of poverty

By way of introduction …

Two countries, worlds apart: one is Korea, an Asian economic powerhouse that's home to industrial giants like Samsung and Hyundai. Its capital, Seoul – once dismissed as "gritty" – has transformed itself and is home to trendy nightlife districts like Garosu-gil and impressive new cultural facilities like the Samsung Foundation. Korean culture isn't just restricted to Seoul: across Asia, young people listen to "K-pop" and flock to Korean movies. Statistics back up the image of a well-off and successful country: Korea's people are healthy – a child born today can expect to live to 80 – and well-educated: 98.5% of the population are in, or have been to school. They're wealthy too: gross domestic product (GDP) per capita stands at over $29 000. On the 2011 United Nations Human Development Index – which comprises measures of health, living standards and education and which is the source for this data (*see box on p. 30*) – Korea ranks 15th in the world.

And then there's Ghana. Its capital, Accra, is also vibrant, and its streets reflect the country's history. Airy, white-bricked buildings are reminders of a colonial past; the broad expanse of Independence Square, with its massive arch, speaks of Ghana's confidence as it gained independence in 1957. Was that confidence justified? Other parts of Accra would seem to suggest not. According to a local official, a third of the city's residents live in slums, while many others live in areas with inadequate access to water and sewerage – a UN Habitat report describes the city as "characterised by choked drains, indiscriminate waste disposal and uncollected refuse in central waste containers." In Ghana, life expectancy is just over 64 years, education enrolment stands at about 56% and GDP per capita is just $1 533 – or around 19 times less than in Korea. On the Human Development Index, Ghana ranks 135th out of 187 countries.

Not much links Korea and Ghana apart from this: in 1957, which is just about two generations ago, with Korea recovering from war and Ghana gaining independence, they were both at about the same level of economic development, with roughly similar levels of GDP per capita. Yet over the years, as the Human Development Index illustrates, these two countries' fates have diverged dramatically, delivering wildly different living standards to their citizens.

It would be easy to leave things there, to sum this up as a story of success vs. failure. But there's a twist in the tale: while Ghana's economic development remains far behind that of Korea, in recent years the country has been quietly turning itself around. Ghana may still be poor, but over the past decade and a half its economy has grown by about 5% a year, investment and exports have both doubled; and the share of people living on less than $1.25 a day – the extreme poverty line – has fallen from about half to just under a third. "Ghana is far from perfect," as Stephen Radelet notes in his book *Emerging Africa*, "but it is much stronger politically, economically and institutionally than it was just 15 years ago."

▶ Why did Korea race ahead of Ghana? And why is Ghana now beginning to justify the confidence it felt at independence? This chapter looks at why some countries grow and some don't. It examines recent shifts in the world economy that have helped to improve the lives of millions, and looks at what we really mean by "poverty". Exploring the true, multidimensional nature of poverty – especially through the lens of the Millennium Development Goals – is essential to understanding the challenge facing development co-operation.

Why are some countries still poor?

A few years ago, James Wolfensohn, a former head of The World Bank, described the progress of the global economy over the previous couple of decades in these terms. The world, he declared, had moved beyond "the old divides of North-South and East-West … it is now rapidly breaking into four tiers of varying levels of prosperity and hope. I call this the Four Speed World."

Wolfensohn described the four speeds of the world economy as follows:

1. **Traditional rich:** The likes of the United States and much of Western Europe, which "for the last 50 years have maintained 80% share of global income while accounting for only 20% of the world's population". These, Wolfensohn forecast, would continue to enjoy improvements in living standards, but would face an increasing contest for dominance from emerging economies.

2. **Emerging:** About 30 poor and middle-income countries, including China and India, which "have learned how to leverage the global economy … [and] will soon become global leaders."

3. **Struggling:** Around 50 countries, Wolfensohn estimated, that "have experienced growth spurts, but also periods of decline or stagnation." Even though home to more than a fifth of the world's population, these countries were "neither poor enough to warrant special aid, nor sufficiently large and fast-growing to be major players in global growth."

4. **Stagnating or declining:** These countries, most in Sub-Saharan Africa, "gain little from globalisation," wrote Wolfensohn, "but are among the most vulnerable to its adverse effects, such as climate change and higher natural resource prices."

Wolfensohn's scheme described what had already happened up to 2007, when he wrote his article; it could not – and did not – aim to forecast what *would* happen. Nevertheless, his way of seeing the world is persuasive, and many people believe he described a process that has essentially continued unabated.

> **"[Wolfensohn's classification] highlights how a group of converging countries are pulling away from the rest of the developing world."**
> *Perspectives on Global Development 2010*

What is that process? Wolfensohn is effectively saying that developing countries have split into two camps – "converging" and "diverging". On the one hand, an increasing number of emerging economies have been converging on the traditional economic powerhouses of the OECD zone. Since the 1990s, the number of such economies has jumped from 12 to 65, according to estimates by the OECD Development Centre. Despite the progress they've made, these economies are still not prosperous, and they remain home to many of the world's poorest people. Also, their development could prove fragile in the face of rising food prices, environmental degradation, or political and economic crises. As shown by both the 2008 global financial crisis and the 2011 turmoil in North Africa and the Middle East, such crises can come with little warning. Nevertheless, and despite the *caveats*, these economies can be said to moving broadly in the right direction.

By contrast, the struggling and declining countries in the bottom categories are diverging: even though they may be seeing some growth, they are slipping further behind the other developing countries. Broadly speaking, these diverging countries are home to the people whom the British economist Paul Collier has described as "the bottom billion". In his influential 2008 book of the same name, Collier warns that these countries are being left behind by globalisation, "falling behind, and often falling apart." Worse still, he argues, their prospects are being hurt by aspects of globalisation. For instance, he argues, the emergence of a global market for workers, especially educated workers such as nurses and engineers, risks robbing the poorest countries of their brightest and best: "In order to turn a country around," Collier writes, "it helps to have a pool of educated people, but the global labour market is draining the bottom billion of their limited pool of such people."

Those who grow, and those who don't

So, if some developing countries have been growing strongly and others have not, it raises an obvious question: Why? The question is simple; the answer is not. The economics profession has long argued over what causes economies to grow and what determines their potential for growth over the long run, but, as *The Economist* puts it, "economists have plenty of theories, but none of them has all the answers".

> "...economic growth is an essential requirement and, frequently, the main contributing factor in reducing income poverty."
>
> *Promoting Pro-Poor Growth: Policy Guidance for Donors*

The issue is important, and not just in the ivory towers of academe. It's true that economic growth does not automatically raise living standards (*see box on p. 30*); on the other hand, it's very difficult to beat poverty in a stagnant or declining economy. Or, to put it another way, "Growth is not an end in itself. But it makes it possible to achieve other important objectives of individuals and societies. It can spare people *en masse* from poverty and drudgery. Nothing else ever has."

That quote comes from the report of the Growth Commission, an international group of experts that came together in 2006 to examine both the real-world experiences of economic growth in recent decades and the state of current thinking on the issue, and to tease out what it might all mean for policy. The commission had plenty of thinking to draw on: particularly since the 1950s, successive economists have examined the growth conundrum. Early work focused on the

2. The persistence of poverty

> ### What are GDP and GNI?
>
> One or two technical terms are unavoidable in discussing economic growth and development. **GDP**, or gross domestic product, is one of them. GDP is a measure – perhaps the standard measure – of the size of a country's economy. More precisely, it represents the scale of total economic activity by essentially calculating the value of the output of all goods and services. (There are a number of different ways of calculating GDP, but they should all produce the same final figure.)
>
> From a development perspective, it's often more helpful to think in terms of **GDP per capita**. Essentially, this represents the GDP figure divided by the size of a country's population, and it gives a relative sense of individuals' economic well-being in a country. To give an example, the IMF estimates that China overtook Japan in 2010 to become the world's second largest economy, with a GDP of $5 745 billion against Japan's $5 391 billion. But because China's population is more than ten times larger than Japan's, China's GDP per capita figure is much, much lower: $3 403 versus Japan's $38 271.
>
> The development world also makes extensive use of another economic measure, **GNI**, or gross national income, and **GNI per capita**. As we've seen, GDP represents the total value of a country's output of goods and services. But the benefits of some economic activity may not always be felt locally; for example, a sneaker manufacturer may send profits back to its overseas parent company. GNI, then, is essentially GDP plus or minus these inflows and outflows.
>
> GNI per capita is used as the basis for The World Bank's widely used classification of countries by income. Updated every year, the classification was as follows in 2011:
> - **Low-income countries (LICs)**: GNI per capita of $1 005 or less, for example Afghanistan, Haiti or Liberia. Among these low-income countries, the United Nations additionally distinguishes 48 as the "least-developed countries", or **LDCs**, which it defines as the world's "poorest and weakest" countries.
> - **Lower middle-income countries (LMICs)**: $1 006 to $3 975; for example, Cameroon, the Philippines or Nicaragua.
> - **Upper middle-income countries (UMICs)**: $3 976 to $12 275, for example China, Mexico and South Africa.
> - **High-income countries (HICs)**: $12 276 or more, for example almost all the OECD countries, Singapore and Saudi Arabia.
>
> Many other terms are used to classify countries in terms of their economic development – **developed, developing, emerging**, and so on, but they have no real fixed definitions. It's common, however, to count almost all high-income developed countries as **developed** and all others as **developing**; **emerging** is often used to describe economies like India, China, Brazil and South Africa that are making substantial economic and social progress.

role – and limits – of investment in infrastructure and the impact of technological change; later, researchers focused increasingly on the impact of innovation and "human capital" – the skills, knowledge, experience and so on – of the workforce; in the 1980s, there was increasing interest in the role of markets and regulation. But, despite all these decades of research, the commission's mission statement acknowledged that there was "growing evidence that the economic and social forces underlying rapid and sustained growth are much less well understood than generally thought". It also conceded that "economic advice to developing countries has been given with more confidence than justified by the state of knowledge."

The Commission's report is interesting because it attempts to take a global view of the factors that favour sustained economic growth – not just purely economic factors but the wider social and political setting. Broadly, it identified five areas of policy that could play a role in sustaining growth:

> **Accumulation**: Investment in things like infrastructure and "human capital" – education, skills, and people's health – the benefits of which may not be felt for years. By its nature, investment means sacrificing an immediate benefit from using resources in favour of a greater return at some stage in the future. Long-term vision is essential to promoting such investment, both by government and the private sector.

> **Innovation**: New things, new ways of doing things and, especially in the context of developing economies, imitation. While people often associate innovation with inventions, like the light bulb or the iPhone, it can also mean developing new systems and processes in everything from agriculture to management. It can also mean learning from industries in other countries. Both China and India have excelled at this – "they imported what the rest of the world knew, and exported what it wanted," as the Growth Commission puts it. Such transfers of knowledge can come in many ways, including by sending people overseas to study and by encouraging foreign direct investment – essentially, companies in one country setting up operations in another.

> **Allocation**: Allowing market forces to play a role in determining how resources are used, rather than relying on central *diktat*. For instance, as economies evolve, some industries stagnate and become increasingly irrelevant. Sustaining such industries can block the entry of newer, more productive companies. Of course, such "creative destruction" comes at a cost, not least the jobs of those working in industries that are no longer viable. Social protection, such as unemployment benefits and healthcare, as well as retraining, can ease such transitions.

2. The persistence of poverty

> ### Who benefits from economic growth?
>
> Economic growth has enormous potential to reduce the effects of poverty and thereby achieve development goals. But economic growth can have possible downsides too, including environmental degradation and growing inequality. In addition, rising national wealth doesn't automatically mean improving living standards: Economies can sometimes grow without delivering much in the way of social improvement. Equally, people's lives can get better even where there is an absence of substantial economic growth.
>
> The Human Development Index is a useful way to think about some of these issues: since 1990, it has measured the progress of countries in three dimensions – health, education and living standards. Analysis of the results from the Index suggest that levels of wealth are indeed associated with levels of education and health – basically, better-off people live longer and spend longer in school. That's not too surprising. But what is perhaps a surprise is that on average *rising* growth is only weakly linked to *improving* health and education. That's not to say that growth doesn't matter: As the *Human Development Report 2010* notes, "Income increases people's command over the resources necessary to gain access to food, shelter, clothing and broader options in life." But it does suggest that there are other ways to deliver improvements. As the report points out, "most countries have the means to improve people's lives."
>
> How? The report notes a number of factors that seem to make a difference.
>
> As a result of globalisation, countries everywhere have the potential to access relatively cheap ideas and innovations that can improve people's lives, for example treating diarrhoea with a simple solution of salt and sugar. However, they differ greatly in the extent to which they actually make use of such ideas. The report suggests that this is due in large part to "variations in institutions and in the underlying social contract". Concretely, where there is a mechanism for holding governments accountable, delivery of healthcare improves. A commitment to equity also seems to matter, not just between rich and poor but between men and women and various social groups.
>
> Economic – and aid – policy can also be directed in ways that deliver more of the fruits of growth to poor people. Again, inclusiveness matters. That means ensuring the poor have access to the economy and receive some support from the state, both in terms of providing basic healthcare and education, and also insulating them from shocks, which can knock back years of progress overnight.

▸ **Stabilisation**: Guarding against inflation, wild swings in currency exchange rates, unpredictable tax burdens. If people and businesses don't know what's going to happen next in an economy, they react rationally by putting off investment. Creating solid institutions can play an important role in helping to stabilise an economy. For instance, a politically independent central bank is usually regarded as key to maintaining inflation targets. Equally, if people trust banks they are more likely to put their money in them rather than storing it under the bed or in the form of jewellery; such savings provide money that can be lent to businesses and entrepreneurs.

> **Inclusion**: Drawing on the reserves of the entire population to drive growth and secure political support by ensuring people don't feel excluded. In many countries, one half of the population – women – are often effectively excluded from economic activity. But exclusion can also affect people living in particular regions or members of certain social groups or tribes. As a result, they may – with good reason – see little reason to support growth strategies. Again, strong institutions can support inclusion, by ensuring that various groups are – and are seen to be – treated fairly and given access to economic opportunity.

Caught in a trap ...

The above list can be thought of as the positive factors that encourage sustainable growth, but it's also possible to look at the problem from the other side – what are the factors that block countries from growing? One of the most influential responses to this question in recent years has come from Paul Collier, who, building on the work of another famous economist, Jeffrey Sachs, has identified a series of "traps" that hold back developing countries, especially in Sub-Saharan Africa. A trap is not just a difficult circumstance, such as an inhospitable climate, but rather a situation that tends to perpetuate itself. Collier gives the example of malaria, a disease that keeps countries poor, "and because they are poor the potential market for a vaccine is not sufficiently valuable to warrant drug companies making the huge investment in research that is necessary."

Collier identifies four traps that keep developing countries poor:

> **Conflict**: Collier argues that three economic factors make countries prone to conflicts like civil war: low income, slow growth and reliance on the export of a commodity like oil. (The latter can both provide a funding source for conflicts, as with the "blood diamonds" in Angola, and spark disputes over control of revenues.) Obviously, war can be devastating not only for societies but also for economies, which only further fuels the factors that lead to conflict in the first place.

> **Natural resources**: Discoveries of oil or diamonds might seem like something to be celebrated, but they often prove to be a curse, not a blessing. Why? There are several reasons.

Economically, they reduce the incentive to develop industries like manufacturing and can also kill off existing manufacturers because of what's sometimes called "Dutch disease" – countries that earn foreign revenue from oil exports can expect to see a rise in the value of their currency, making their non-oil exports costlier. And because commodity prices tend to fluctuate quite widely, they can also create economic instability. Politically, governments that rely on oil revenues can be less accountable than those that rely on tax revenues. While few citizens enjoy paying tax, it does at least create an expectation that governments will be open about how they spend all that tax money. As a result, money is less likely to be wasted and is more likely to be put to productive ends.

> **Landlocked, and with bad neighbours**: The experience of countries like Botswana or Switzerland might suggest that being landlocked is no obstacle to success. But, Collier believes it is, and estimates that just under two out of five of the "bottom billion" live in countries without direct access to the sea. That leaves them dependent on the state of their neighbours' infrastructure and political stability to get their exports out to the world. While there's little a country can do about geography without starting a war, Collier argues it can compensate in other ways, for instance by becoming a regional centre for finance, telecommunications, pushing for regional development, and making itself attractive to donors. Few of these steps can be taken, however, in the absence of good governance.

> **Bad governance**: Collier argues that good governance can take a country only so far – sustainable economic growth can't go beyond a certain level, perhaps around 10% a year, no matter how much the quality of governance improves. On the other hand, there's almost no limit to the damage that can be caused by bad governance – a country can rapidly go from economic decline to becoming an outright failed state. Recovery can take decades.

Again, as with the Growth Commission's report, it's interesting to note Collier's emphasis on governance issues – a concern that's been increasingly echoed among donor and developing countries in recent years, and one that we will return to later in this book. Among the signs of that growing interest is a large increase in spending to strengthen governance in what are known as "fragile states" – states that OECD defines as "failing to provide basic services to poor people because they are unwilling or unable to do so". Such states are home to many – but by no means all – of the world's poorest people, and form a major part of the development challenge. But what is that challenge? In the next, and last, section of this chapter, we'll look at the scale of poverty in the world today.

> "Achieving the Millennium Development Goals will depend on how successful we are at helping the world's most fragile states. This group of 48 countries represents the poorest of the poor, often because of violent conflict and poor governance."
>
> *Development Co-operation Report 2010*

What is the development challenge?

People sometimes think of poverty solely in terms of material wealth, or the lack of it. Indeed, one of the most widely used measures of it is the number of people living on $1.25 a day or less – The World Bank's extreme poverty line. (This is also sometimes referred to as "absolute poverty" or "dollar a day" poverty.) On that measure, the news on poverty in recent decades has been very good: the percentage of people on the poverty line worldwide fell from 46% in 1990 to 27% in 2005 (the most recent year for which comprehensive global data is available). On current trends, and even taking account of the impact of the global recession in 2009, that percentage should fall to below 15% by 2015. If that happens, the number of people living in absolute poverty will have fallen from 1.8 billion in 1990 to half that number, 900 million, in 2015, achieving the MDG poverty reduction goal, and that's against the background of a substantial rise in the world population.

But poverty is not simply about income and wealth. It's also about resources – access to things like clean water, food, education and basic healthcare, without which people face an uphill struggle to improve their standard of living and quality of life. These core dimensions of poverty can be thought of in the following ways, based on guidelines from the OECD:

- ➤ **Economic:** The ability to earn an income, to consume and to have assets, as well as secure access to resources like land, tools and animals, forests and fishing waters, credit and a job.

> **Human well-being:** Health, education, nutrition, clean water and shelter.
> **Political:** Human rights, a voice and some influence over public policies and political priorities, and basic political freedoms, including from arbitrary, unjust and violent action by the state and its representatives.
> **Socio-cultural:** The ability to participate as a valued member of a community, reflecting conditions like social status and dignity. In some societies, factors like caste, occupation or geographical location can effectively lead to people's social and economic exclusion.
> **Protective capabilities:** The ability to withstand economic and external shocks, including illness, crime, war and destitution.

All these dimensions of poverty are also interlinked with gender inequality, because poverty doesn't affect men and women in the same ways, and with environmental degradation, which can be both a cause and consequence of poverty.

This "multidimensionality" of poverty is formally recognised in a number of key international indicators, such as the United Nations' Human Development Index, which combines data on income as well as life expectancy (representing health) and education levels to produce a composite figure representing each country's level of development. The index also includes a section examining multidimensional poverty: in the 104 countries covered, the number of people who are poor in terms of lacking resources is higher than the number living on the poverty line, 1.75 billion vs. 1.44 billion.

> "The concept of poverty includes different dimensions of deprivation. In general, it is the inability of people to meet economic, social and other standards of well-being."
> DAC Guidelines on Poverty Reduction, 2001

The need to see poverty in a wider context is also reflected in the Millennium Development Goals (MDGs), which set targets not just for reducing income poverty but also for increasing education levels and improving access to water, among others. As the next few pages show, the MDGs also provide a useful lens for understanding the extent of poverty – and, to a large extent, the scale of the global challenge for development co-operation.

The Millennium Development Goals

The MDGs trace their roots to a troubled time in development. By the mid-1990s, aid from developed countries was declining and the needs of traditional recipient countries were being eclipsed by the problems of states in the former Soviet bloc. Among members of the OECD's DAC, there was a desire for a "new vision that would sustain the relevance of development assistance in a rapidly changing world", as Richard Manning, a former chairman of the DAC, has written. That determination led to a decision to set some striking targets against which the progress of development could be measured.

Goals and targets weren't new in development circles. They had featured in the outputs from a series of UN-backed conferences in the early to mid-1990s, and were valued for introducing a sense of urgency and for providing a reference against which accomplishment could be compared. The DAC took this work as the foundation for building a concise set of development goals, and then went further: most striking, perhaps, it set an ambitious target to reduce by half the number of people living in absolute poverty by 2015.

Adopted early in the new millennium, the MDGs set out eight targets for combating poverty to be reached by 2015. If all eight Goals were fully attained – which currently seems unlikely – it would mark a major step forward in poverty reduction. But by improving things like health and education levels, it would also build firm foundations for future development. The Goals are thus integral to understanding the current scale of poverty – in all its dimensions – and the development challenge facing the world today.

The probability that the MDGs won't be met in full has led to some cynicism about their role. But there's little doubt they have had a lasting impact. Perhaps one of the most significant is the way they've reshaped the development debate. They have, as *The Economist* has stated, managed to "shift the debate away from how much is being spent on development to how much is being achieved".

The structure of the MDGs is a little more complex than it might seem at first sight. While most coverage focuses on the idea of the eight goals, in reality there are a number of sub-targets for several of the goals. For example, Goal 1 sets targets for three distinct but related areas: poverty, hunger and jobs. All told, there are 21 headline targets in the Goals, underlining the idea that poverty has many dimensions. Over the next few pages, we'll examine the challenge for development co-operation in the early 21st century through the lens of the MDGs.

2. The persistence of poverty

GOAL 1: ERADICATE POVERTY AND HUNGER

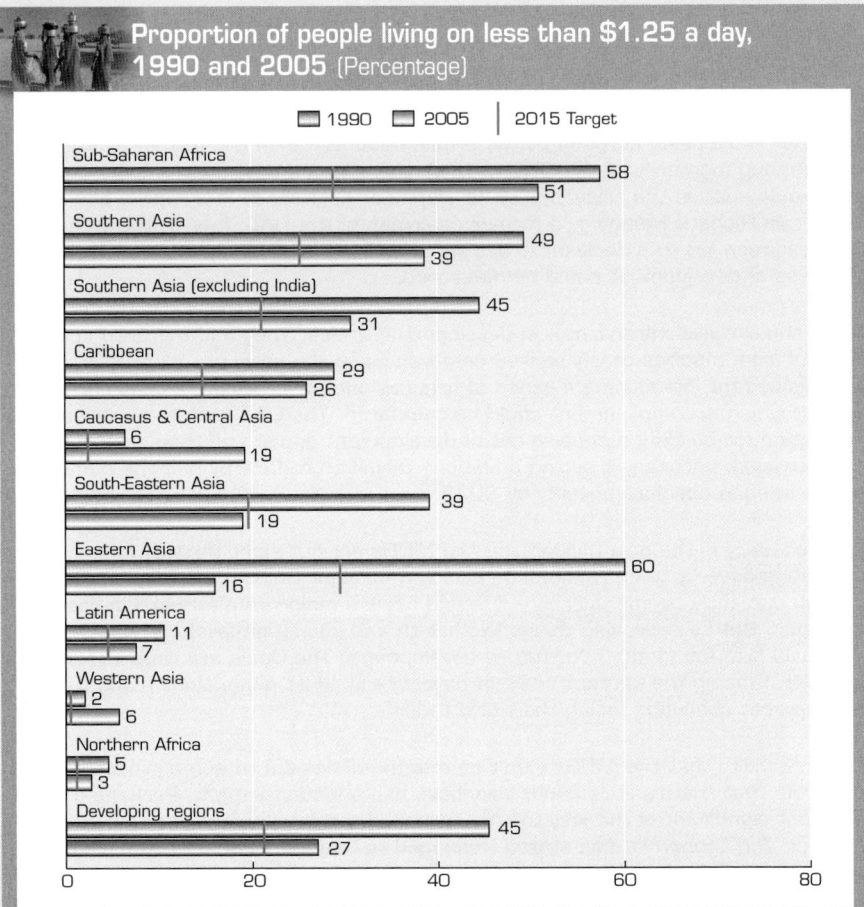

Proportion of people living on less than $1.25 a day, 1990 and 2005 (Percentage)

The proportion of people living on or below the poverty line ($1.25 a day) has fallen substantially since 1990 in most of the world, although there are exceptions, most notably Central Asia. The region with the highest *proportion* of people living in absolute poverty is Sub-Saharan Africa. But in absolute terms, a case can be made for saying that more of the world's poor live in Southern Asia, especially India, which is classed as a middle-income country. British researcher Andy Sumner argues that about three-quarters of the world's 1.3 billion poorest people live today in what The World Bank classes as middle-income countries. He contrasts this "new bottom billion" with the 1990s, when almost all the world's poorest people (93%) lived in low-income countries.

Source: UN (2011), *The Millennium Development Goals Report 2011.*

GOAL 1: ERADICATE POVERTY AND HUNGER

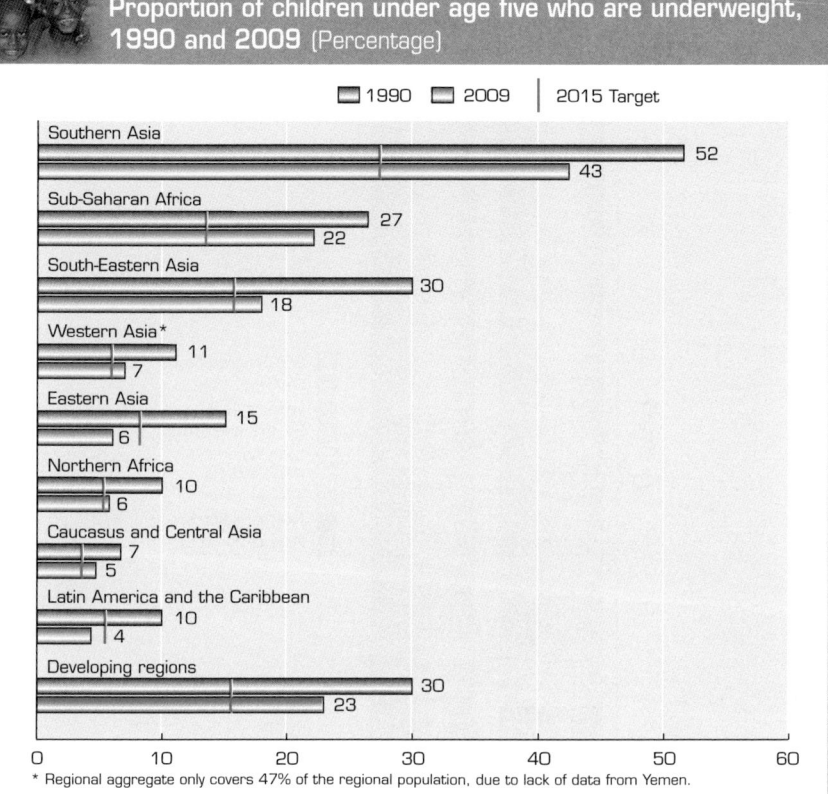

Proportion of children under age five who are underweight, 1990 and 2009 (Percentage)

Region	1990	2009
Southern Asia	52	43
Sub-Saharan Africa	27	22
South-Eastern Asia	30	18
Western Asia*	11	7
Eastern Asia	15	6
Northern Africa	10	6
Caucasus and Central Asia	7	5
Latin America and the Caribbean	10	4
Developing regions	30	23

* Regional aggregate only covers 47% of the regional population, due to lack of data from Yemen.

Hunger has an immediate impact on people's lives by sapping them of energy to work or study. It can also have a lingering effect: pregnant women who are hungry are more likely to have underweight or sickly babies, while hungry children develop more slowly. Around one in four children in developing countries were undernourished in 2009, the most recent year for which data is available. More recently, the United Nations' Food and Agriculture Organization estimates that just under a billion people, or 925 million, were probably undernourished in 2010. That represents about 16% of the world's population, slightly down on the figure of 20% in the very early 1990s. However, the progress that's been made in recent decades may be increasingly hard to sustain in the face of rising food prices. Goal 1 also covers employment: job prospects for poor people, especially women and young people, were hit by the economic crisis of 2008.

Source: UN (2011), *The Millennium Development Goals Report 2011*.

GOAL 2: UNIVERSAL EDUCATION

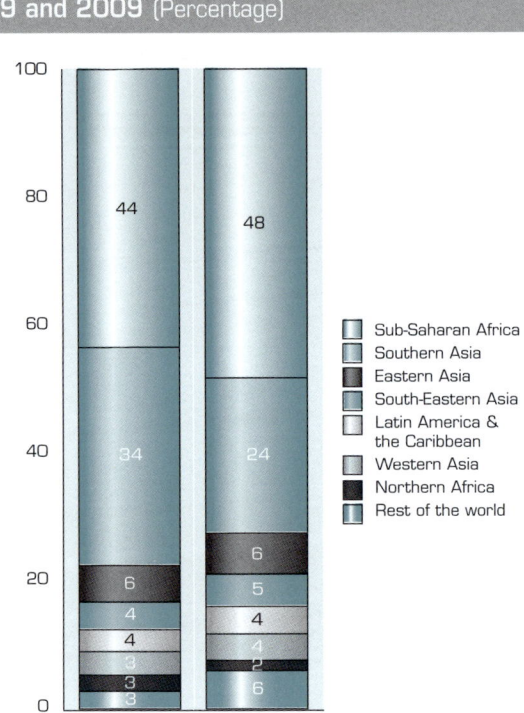

Distribution of out-of-school children by region, 1999 and 2009 (Percentage)

- Sub-Saharan Africa
- Southern Asia
- Eastern Asia
- South-Eastern Asia
- Latin America & the Caribbean
- Western Asia
- Northern Africa
- Rest of the world

Education is a key foundation stone for individual economic success. Around the world, people who've been to school earn more and have better job prospects. Education is also a key driver of national economic success, and brings social benefits, too. Enrolment in primary education has risen across developing countries, and stood at about 89% in 2009. Between 1999 and 2009, the number of school-age children who weren't getting an education fell from 106 million to 67 million. As the chart shows, most of them were living in one of two regions: Sub-Saharan Africa (32 million children out of school) and South Asia (16 million). Children from the poorest families are least likely to go to school. In much of the developing world, children in the countryside are also less likely to go to school than their urban peers. Despite rising enrolment, there's concern that the quality of education in some developing countries is poor. In India, for example, it's estimated that only about half of enrolled children can read at first-grade level.

Source: UN (2011), The Millennium Development Goals Report 2011.

GOAL 3: GENDER EQUALITY

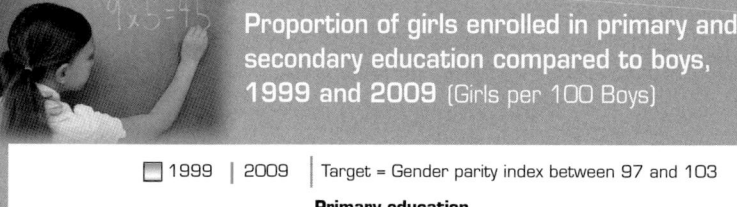

Proportion of girls enrolled in primary and secondary education compared to boys, 1999 and 2009 (Girls per 100 Boys)

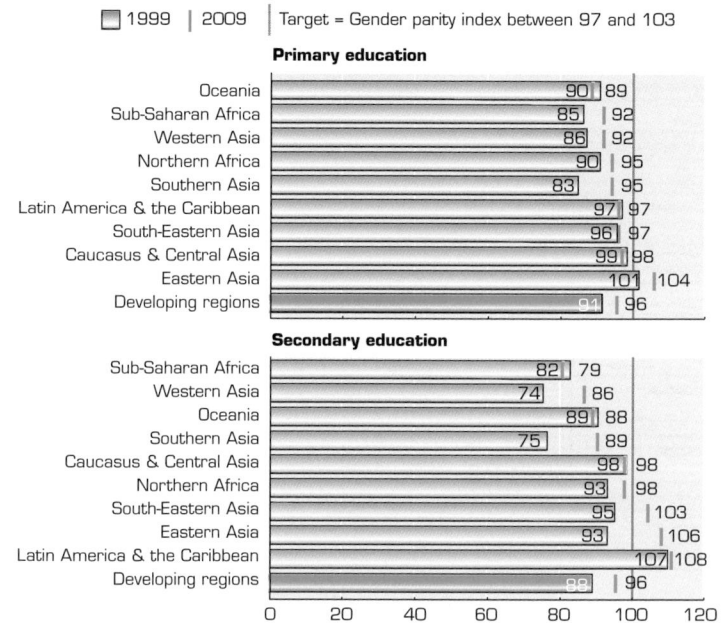

Girls and women face discrimination across their lives, not least in education and employment. This has knock-on effects across society, reducing living standards not just for women but for their families, and depriving economies of a vital source of labour and entrepreneurship. In education, girls from the poorest families remain the least likely group to attend school, as the chart shows. Overall, however, there's been substantial improvement in girls' education prospects. In developing countries in 1999, there were 91 girls for every 100 boys enrolled in primary schools; by 2009, that had risen to 96 girls for every 100 boys. At secondary level, the improvement was even stronger: in 1999 there were 88 girls for 100 boys; by 2009, that had risen to 96 girls for 100 boys. Outside education, women are seriously underrepresented in the workforce, and in parliament, in many parts of the world: in southern and western Asia and northern Africa, women account for just one in five workers in non-agricultural jobs.

Source: UN (2011), *The Millennium Development Goals Report 2011.*

GOAL 4: CHILD HEALTH

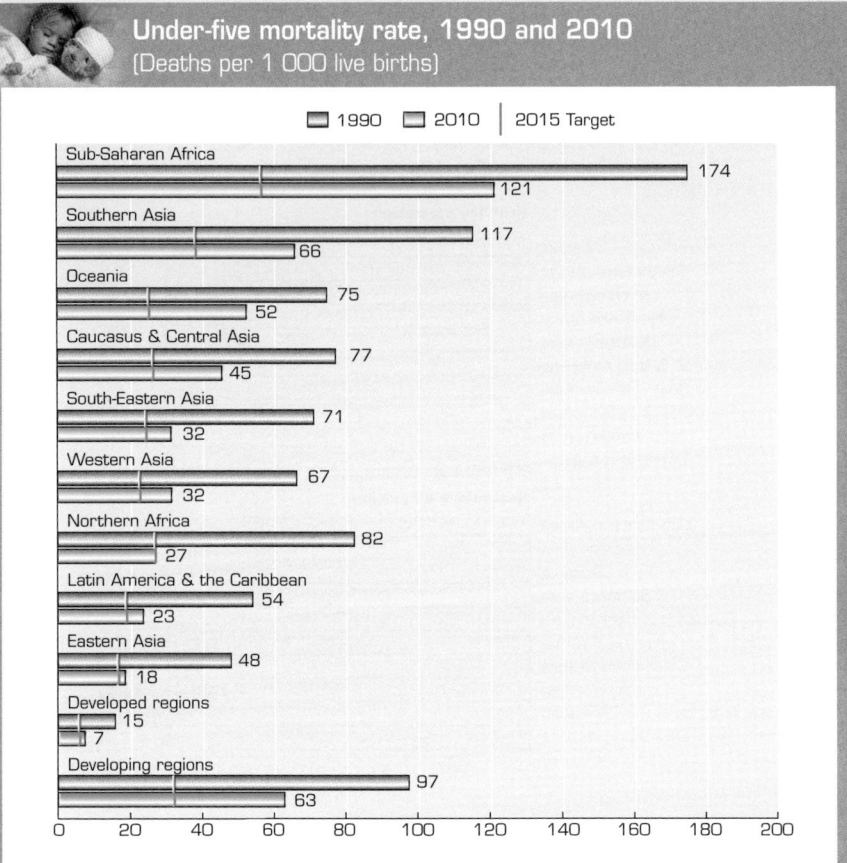

The death of a young child is a tragedy for its family. In economic terms, it can also represent a drain on its resources. Mortality rates for under-5s also offer an insight into the overall health of children in a country or region. As the chart shows, deaths among the under-5s have fallen in much of the world; however, the goal of reducing such deaths by two-thirds by 2015 can only be met if substantial and accelerated action is taken to eliminate the leading killers of children. Just four diseases account for more than two-fifths of child mortality: pneumonia, diarrhoea, malaria and AIDS. Many of these deaths could be prevented easily and relatively cheaply. For example, encouraging mothers to breastfeed gives infants very strong protection against diarrhoea; educating parents in healthy toilet habits also goes a long way to keeping kids safe; and if children do fall ill, they can often be treated cheaply and effectively with a simple solution of salt and sugar.

Source: UN (2011), *The Millennium Development Goals Report 2011, Addendum-Goal 4.*

GOAL 5: MATERNAL HEALTH

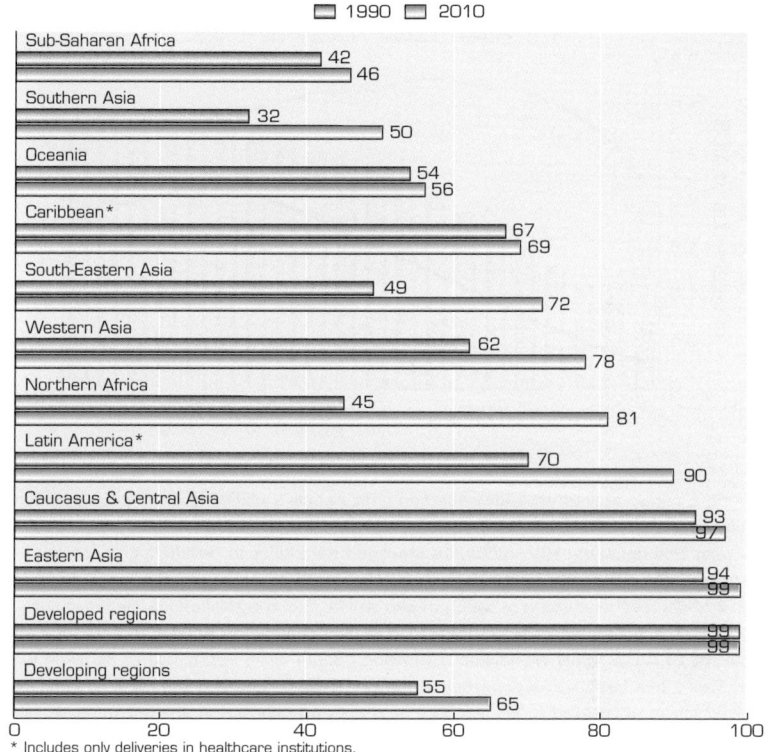

Proportion of deliveries attended by skilled health personnel, 1990 and 2010
(Percentage)

Region	1990	2010
Sub-Saharan Africa	42	46
Southern Asia	32	50
Oceania	54	56
Caribbean*	67	69
South-Eastern Asia	49	72
Western Asia	62	78
Northern Africa	45	81
Latin America*	70	90
Caucasus & Central Asia	93	97
Eastern Asia	94	99
Developed regions	99	99
Developing regions	55	65

* Includes only deliveries in healthcare institutions.

The presence of a trained healthcare worker during delivery is crucial in reducing maternal deaths. Despite improvements in some regions, notably Northern Africa, women in many developing countries still give birth without professional medical assistance. In Sub-Saharan Africa, more than half of women give birth without the assistance of trained medical workers. The proportions are even higher in rural areas, where poor road conditions and lack of transport make it difficult to rush emergency cases to hospital. The problems reflect a mix of factors, including lack of facilities and mothers' low levels of education. "There are delays at facilities and still many myths about hospital births," Zambian midwife Rosemary Kabwe told *The Guardian*. "For example, women don't want male doctors or are scared that the placenta won't be disposed of properly. We urgently need more midwives and better record-keeping. Women are dying quietly and unnoticed."

Source: UN (2011), *The Millennium Development Goals Report 2011.*

GOAL 6: COMBAT HIV/AIDS

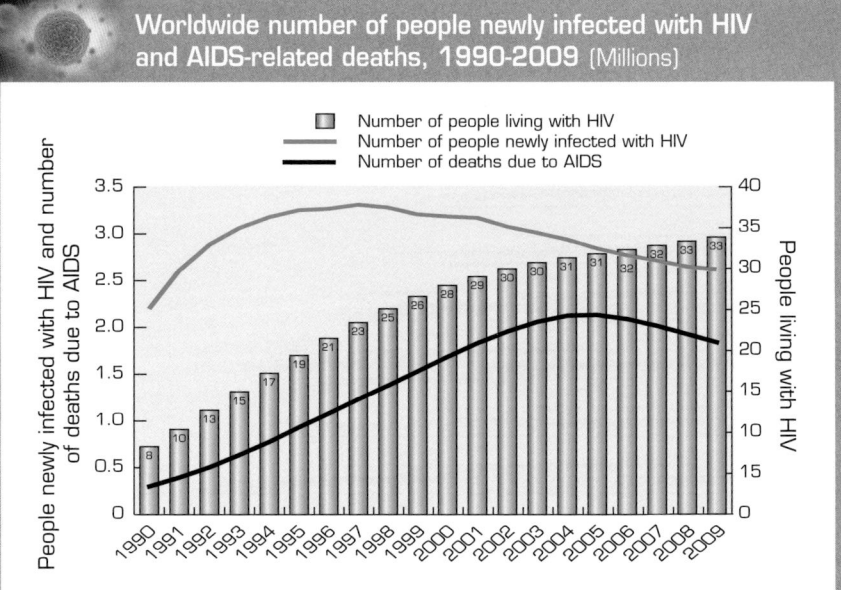

Worldwide number of people newly infected with HIV and AIDS-related deaths, 1990-2009 (Millions)

Among a range of ill-effects, disease can limit people's ability to earn a living, drain family resources, and hold back children's physical and mental development. Over the past few decades, HIV/AIDS has emerged as a killer in developing countries, claiming 2.2 million lives at its peak in 2004. Death rates have fallen back since then, with the disease stabilising in much of the world, but the challenges remain acute. In 2009, for instance, an estimated 14.8 million children in Sub-Saharan Africa lost a parent to AIDS, while worldwide 33 million people were estimated to be living with HIV. There has been some progress in fighting other diseases, too. A fivefold increase in production of treated mosquito nets is improving protection against malaria, which claimed an estimated 781 000 lives in 2009. Tuberculosis prevalence is also falling back somewhat, although the disease still killed an estimated 1.7 million people in 2009.

Source: UN (2011), The Millennium Development Goals Report 2011.

2. The persistence of poverty

GOAL 7: ENVIRONMENTAL SUSTAINABILITY

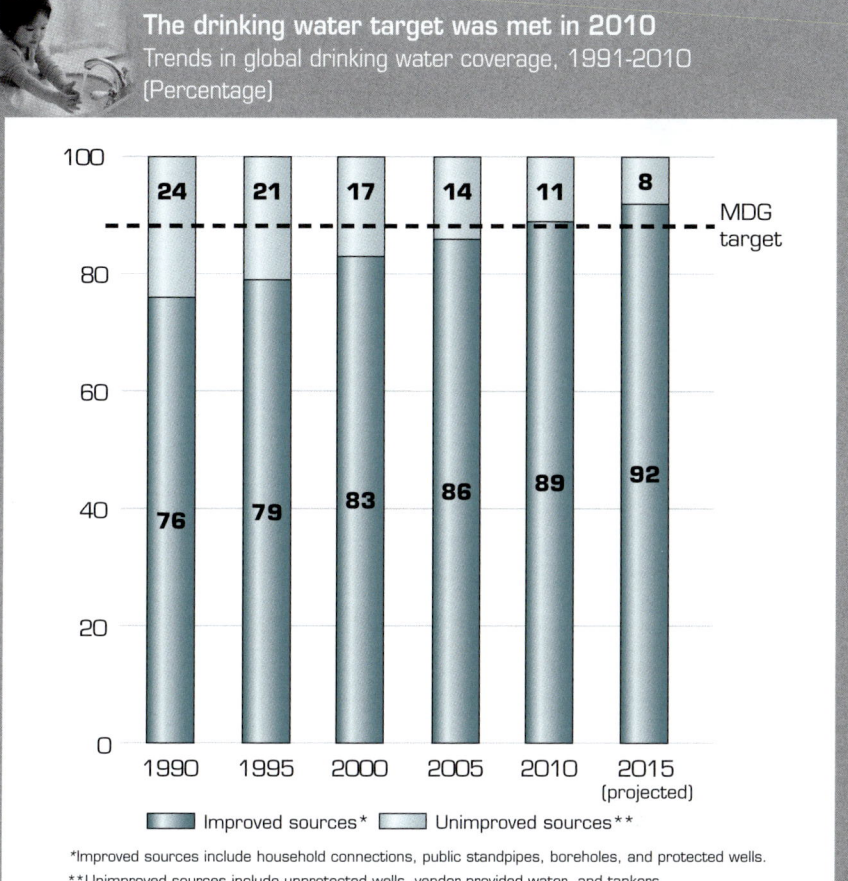

The drinking water target was met in 2010
Trends in global drinking water coverage, 1991-2010
(Percentage)

Year	Improved sources*	Unimproved sources**
1990	76	24
1995	79	21
2000	83	17
2005	86	14
2010	89	11
2015 (projected)	92	8

MDG target

*Improved sources include household connections, public standpipes, boreholes, and protected wells.
**Unimproved sources include unprotected wells, vendor provided water, and tankers.

The MDG 7 target of halving the proportion of the population without sustainable access to safe drinking water between 1990 and 2015 has been met, but 780 million people remain without access, and coverage is only 63% in the least developed countries. Moreover, the world is unlikely to achieve the objective of 75% access to improved sanitation such as through flush toilets. Other targets that may be missed include preserving biodiversity and habitats for threatened species. Deforestation has slowed, but remains worryingly high in South America and Africa. Action to reduce carbon emissions, blamed for causing climate change, is urgently needed.

Source: UNICEF and WHO (2012), *Progress on Drinking Water and Sanitation, 2012 Update.*

2. The persistence of poverty

GOAL 8: GLOBAL PARTNERSHIP FOR DEVELOPMENT

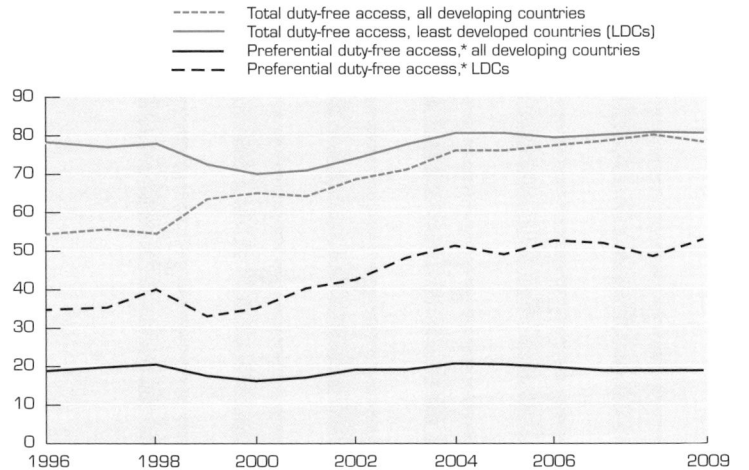

Proportion of developed country imports from developing countries and from the LDCs admitted free of duty, 1996-2009 (Percentage)

* Preferential duty-free access is calculated by subtracting from the total duty-free access all products receiving duty free treatment under the most-favoured-nation treatment (MFN) regime.

The last of the eight MDGs examines the extent to which developing and developed countries are working together to bring about development. It covers a number of areas, including aid provision and whether or not donors are meeting aid commitments, as well as the extent to which developing countries have access to new technologies and to global markets. Around 60% of the world's Internet users were in developing countries in 2010, but this represents just 21% of their population. Duty-free imports by developed countries from developing countries have risen substantially, hitting almost 80% in 2009, up from 54% in 1998. However, less encouragingly, the continuing failure to reach agreement on the Doha trade round – which was intended to improve access for developing countries to world markets – means there's been relatively little progress in this area in recent years.

Source: UN (2011), *The Millennium Development Goals Report 2011*.

Find Out More

FROM OECD...

On the Internet

To find out more about the **Millennium Development Goals**, including the OECD's role in helping to bring them about, go to *www.oecd.org/dac/mdg*. For information on OECD work on poverty reduction, go to *www.oecd.org/dac/poverty*.

The crisis convinced many countries that a different kind of economic growth is needed, which takes into account environmental, social and technological considerations. For information on **OECD work on green growth**, go to: *www.oecd.org/greengrowth*.

Publications

Perspectives on Global Development (series): From the OECD's Development Centre, this series aims to describe and analyse changes in the global economy and the impact of these on the world's developing countries. The 2010 edition, *Shifting Wealth*, focuses on the major realignment of the global economy that has taken place in the last two decades, which has seen increased economic and political power shifts towards the developing world and emerging economies. The 2012 edition, *Social Cohesion in a Shifting World,* looks at ways to build cohesive societies in this changing global context.

Natural Resources and Pro-Poor Growth: The Economics and Politics (2009): This book demonstrates that natural resources can contribute to growth, employment, exports and fiscal revenues in low-income countries, where natural capital constitutes a quarter of total wealth. It highlights the importance of policies encouraging the sustainable management of these resources, and emphasises the need to address the political challenges of natural-resource management for long-term pro-poor economic growth.

Promoting Pro-poor Growth: Policy Guidance for Donors (2007): This volume identifies the restraints that limit the impact of development initiatives in reducing poverty, and offers policies and strategies to address them. The recommendations, which focus particularly on the roles of private sector development, agriculture and infrastructure, aim to help change donor behaviour and pave the way for more effective development co-operation.

DAC Guidelines on Poverty Reduction (2001): These guidelines provide practical information about the nature of poverty and best-practice approaches, policies, instruments and channels for tackling it. They set out the parameters for building effective partnerships with governments, civil society, and other development actors.

Shaping the 21st Century (1996) (*www.oecd.org/dataoecd/23/35/2508761.pdf*): A landmark report from the OECD's Development Assistance Committee, which laid the foundations for the Millennium Development Goals and, ultimately, the Paris Declaration on Aid Effectiveness, both of which have become cornerstones of development co-operation in the 21st century.

... AND OTHER SOURCES

We Can End Poverty (*www.un.org/millenniumgoals*): A portal for the full range of UN work on achieving and monitoring the Millennium Development Goals.

Human Development Report (*http://hdr.undp.org/en*): This editorially independent report was established by the United Nations in 1990 with the aim of putting people at the heart of the development debate. It's partnered with the **Human Development Index** (*http://hdr.undp.org/en/statistics*), which ranks countries along three dimensions of development: Health, Education and Living Standards.

3

Aid is a big part of the world's development co-operation effort. Most comes from developed countries, but China and countries in the Arab world are also significant contributors, as are multilateral bodies like The World Bank, as well as **NGOs** and billionaires like Bill Gates.

What is aid?

3. What is aid?

By way of introduction ...

Shortly before 5 o'clock on a Tuesday afternoon in January 2010, an earthquake struck Haiti. The impact was immediate and appalling: "Everything started shaking, people were screaming, houses started collapsing," a Reuters reporter said. "I saw people under the rubble, and people killed. People were screaming 'Jesus, Jesus' and running in all directions."

The quake, one of the most severe in recent memory, claimed more than 300 000 lives, according to Haiti's government, although some other estimates indicate the toll was lower. At the height of the ensuing crisis, estimates of the numbers of homeless reached as high as 1.5 million people. The disaster provoked an immediate response from the international community, and teams of aid workers, soldiers and medical officials began arriving on the island within hours of the earthquakes. "We are working like crazy," wrote one, Emerson Tan. "Everyone very tired and filthy. Racing against the clock. ... UK team had some successes but one agonising failure when an 18-year-old girl died minutes away from rescue. Too busy to be sad ... "

Ask most people to define foreign aid, and they will probably point to scenes such as these. That's probably not too surprising: news about earthquakes and natural disasters can dominate the headlines for days and weeks, producing a flood of stark and disturbing images. But the reality of aid is rather different. In fact, the sort of emergency aid that flowed into Haiti forms only a very small slice of development assistance: it rarely accounts for more than about one in ten dollars provided by governments in aid, and often much less. Unlike emergency aid, which may be provided at very short notice, most aid is planned out over a much longer timeframe, and is aimed at building long-term foundations for development rather than relieving short-term distress.

▶ This chapter introduces some of the key terms used to describe the complex world of aid and assistance. It explores the sorts of aid provided to developing countries, and introduces some of the key players in the aid world, including government and non-government agencies.

Is all aid the same?

So, what is aid? The question is simple, the answer is not. Where aid is discussed in this book, the focus is mainly on what's known as Official Development Assistance, or ODA, which in very basic terms is aid from governments in developed countries to developing countries. This is not the only form of support they provide, but it's by far the biggest single category. We'll examine ODA first, and then look briefly at some other forms of assistance, both from government and non-government sources.

Understanding Official Development Assistance (ODA)

Twenty-three developed countries – as well as the European Union – sit on the OECD's Development Assistance Committee (DAC), and they provide the bulk of the world's official assistance. Their aid, as well as aid from 20 other countries and all the main multilateral aid agencies, is monitored by the OECD. While the OECD collects data on all resource flows for development – including private investment and philanthropy – the main emphasis is on ODA. In simple terms, ODA has three key characteristics:

> It comes from governments, either at national or state level, or from their official agencies;

> It's targeted at improving the economic development and welfare of developing countries; and

> It's either a grant, or a loan at a rate less than market interest rates.

Let's look a little more closely at some of these characteristics, as well as at a few terms that turn up regularly in discussions of ODA, some of which we'll look at in greater detail later in this book:

Loan or grant: About 90% of ODA is made up of grants, in other words it's money that the developing country won't have to repay. Much of the rest is made up of loans, but these are not loans charged at bank or money-market rates. Rather, they are "concessional" – or "soft" – loans, charged at below-market rates and often with a longer repayment period. It might seem strange to ask a relatively poor country to repay assistance, but such lending can be seen as a way of introducing greater accountability and responsibility into development financing. And if the investment made with the loan generates higher returns than the interest rate paid, then it's a good deal for the country concerned.

Planned or emergency: Emergency aid gets much of the world's media attention, but in reality most ODA is planned out in advance and is not triggered by emergencies such as the 2004 Asian tsunami or the 2010 Haiti earthquake. Indeed, in 2008 emergency relief accounted for only about 3% of ODA, although the proportion has been much higher in years of cataclysmic events.

Debt forgiveness: Donor countries sometimes agree to defer loan repayments or cancel them altogether. Cancellations are recorded as "grants" in ODA, even though, in effect, no new funding is being provided at the time when the loan is forgiven. The chart (*p. 51*) shows a large spike in debt forgiveness in the mid-2000s, which followed the successful Jubilee 2000 campaign to forgive developing countries' debt. Most of the loans forgiven were not aid in the first place; typically, for example, they may have originally been export credits. But loan forgiveness frees resources for developing countries to use as they wish, and so is counted as ODA.

Bilateral or multilateral: ODA is "bilateral" when it's given directly by the donor country to people or institutions in the recipient country. It's multilateral when it's provided to an international agency, such as the United Nations. From the donors' perspective, about 70% of ODA is bilateral and 30% multilateral. The agencies decide how to spend the multilateral money. But they also receive "earmarked" money. Because the donors to a large extent tell the agencies how to use these earmarked funds, they are counted within bilateral aid. Counting this earmarked or "multi-bi" funding, multilateral agencies actually deliver about 40% of total aid.

Technical co-operation: Technical co-operation takes two main forms: the first involves paying for training for people from developing countries, both at home and abroad, often by providing study scholarships. The second, and perhaps the more widely used form, involves supplying consultants, advisors, teachers and administrators to developing countries. The intervention of such outsiders can provide much-needed expertise and experience, but the practice is also widely criticised – an OECD report referred to it as "perhaps the most controversial type of aid". Foreign experts may be resented by locals, in part because of a

3. What is aid?

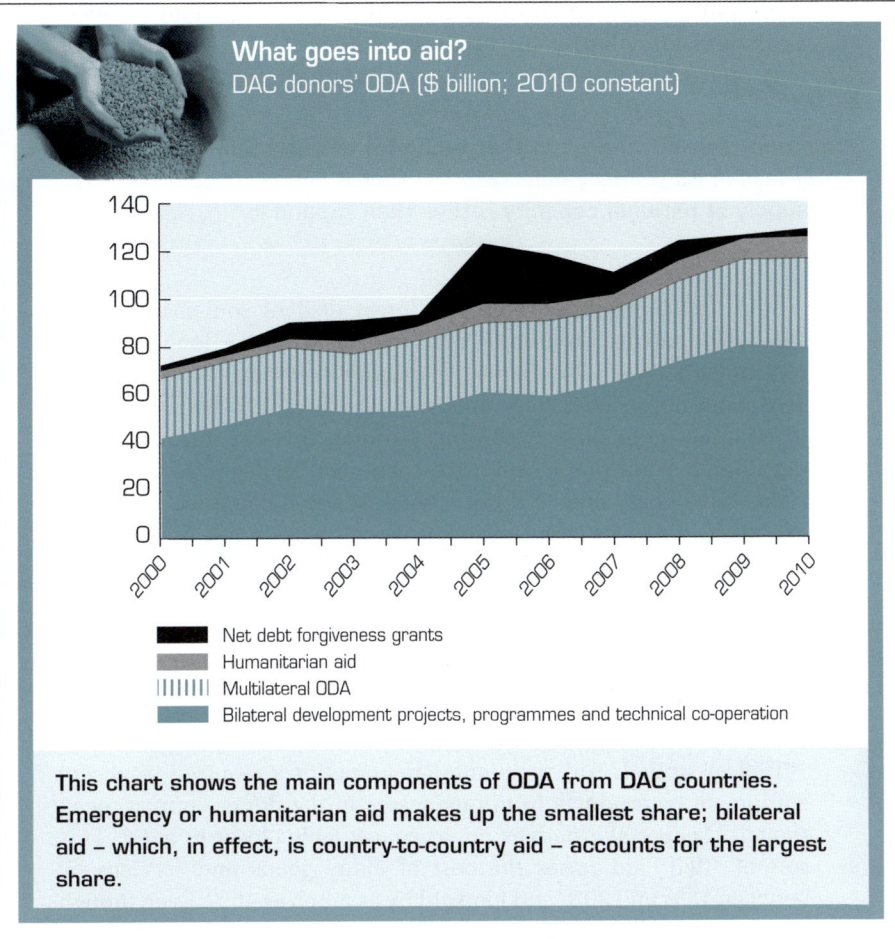

What goes into aid?
DAC donors' ODA ($ billion; 2010 constant)

- Net debt forgiveness grants
- Humanitarian aid
- Multilateral ODA
- Bilateral development projects, programmes and technical co-operation

This chart shows the main components of ODA from DAC countries. Emergency or humanitarian aid makes up the smallest share; bilateral aid – which, in effect, is country-to-country aid – accounts for the largest share.

Source: OECD, 6 April 2011; www.oecd.org/dataoecd/54/41/47515917.pdf
StatLink: http://dx.doi.org/10.1787/888932606188

perception – sometimes justified – that they are overpaid: "When Australia posted civil servants from various departments to assist the government of Papua New Guinea in 2004, the total bill for some of them reached over $500 000 annually – almost 10 times their gross pay at home," the *Development Co-operation Report 2005* noted. They have also at times been accused of introducing technologies and approaches that are inappropriate to developing countries' needs. More broadly, technical co-operation has been criticised for failing to contribute to the development of local skills and knowledge: for example, students who train oversees may opt to stay there, thus fuelling a "brain drain" of talent.

> "…a more serious charge is that technical co-operation often fails in its primary objective, i.e. that it can restrict the supply of national capacity rather than expand it."
>
> Development Co-operation Report 2005

Such criticisms have sparked a great deal of soul-searching in the development community over the years, and a long series of recommendations for better managing technical co-operation. Two main approaches have emerged. The first is to hand the reins to recipient countries. Regarding training, this can mean helping developing countries to improve their own colleges so that they train students at home and not abroad. When it comes to supplying expertise, it can be more effective if recipients – not donors – do the hiring. The second approach is to make better use of existing knowledge. Rather than parachuting in foreign experts, developing countries can be encouraged to make better use of existing skills, institutions and economic structures. As we'll see in Chapter 8, there's also growing interest in encouraging dialogue *between* developing countries to exchange ideas, experiences and lessons learnt.

Tied or untied: Aid recipients are sometimes required to accept equipment or products from businesses in the donor country, even though cheaper alternatives might be available closer to hand. This sort of "tied" aid raises the cost of many goods and services by between 15% and 30% and food aid by as much as 40%. Even though tying makes aid less effective, it was sometimes defended in the past as necessary to build support for aid programmes in donor countries. The OECD led a long-running campaign to persuade donors to untie aid, and by 2007 about four-fifths of ODA was untied.

Conditionality: In basic terms, this is aid with "strings attached". To receive, or go on receiving aid, developing countries typically have to commit to making certain reforms, for example liberalising the economy, reforming governance, or eliminating corruption. Conditionality is highly controversial and there's a great deal of debate over what it achieves. Advocates say it's a useful incentive for driving reform in developing countries and a way to increase accountability. Opponents say there's limited evidence that it does actually lead to reforms. They also say that donors often fail to follow up on whether conditions have been met, thereby limiting the impact on accountability.

Project, programme or budget support: In the early days, most aid money went to specified projects, the building of a bridge, for instance, or a road or hospital. Such projects were often high-profile, and appeared to offer visible evidence that aid was working. But there were problems. For one thing, the lengthy planning needed for some of these projects tied up aid commitments for long periods, and reduced flexibility when it came to responding to new needs. For another, one-off projects weren't always well integrated into national systems – as one aid veteran told the author, "we were building schools, not education systems". Lack of follow-up sometimes meant that hospitals were built, but lacked the funds or resources to perform operations. And while it was relatively easy to measure the direct impact of such projects, it was less easy to get a sense of their wider economic effects.

From the 1980s, aid became more programme-based, and better integrated within the recipient government's own spending programmes, ensuring those governments have more say over how to spend it. In basic terms, there are two main approaches. In the first, sometimes called the sector-wide approach, or SWAp, donors – often working as a group – decide to support a sector such as education, health or water supply, and donate funds to help meet the recipient government's own goals in the sector. The second approach, budget support, occurs when donors contribute aid to the recipient government's overall coffers, allowing it to raise spending overall. Today, most substantial projects are better integrated into developing countries' own expenditure programmes. In 2008, a little over half of bilateral ODA was classed as "Country Programmable Aid", or CPA, the portion of aid that each donor can programme for each recipient country.

Other forms of aid

ODA from developed countries is not the only form that aid takes. As we'll see in the next section, in broad terms there are two other major sources: the first is private philanthropy, which includes charities, non-governmental and civil society organisations – think of the Gates Foundation, Médecins Sans Frontières ("Doctors without Borders") and Oxfam International. The second is government, or official, assistance from countries that are not members of the OECD Development Assistance Committee (DAC), such as countries in the Arab world and emerging economies like China, India and Brazil. Collectively, countries in this latter group are sometimes referred to as the **new development partners**.

ODA represents the largest single component of aid, but exact comparisons between it and other forms are hard to come by: ODA is reliably measured by government statistical agencies and the OECD, but there are gaps in measuring other assistance. Nevertheless, researchers led by development veteran Homi Kharas have come up with some estimates for the scale of each aid flow. Their work suggests – as many people suspect – that although ODA is still the largest slice of the aid cake, its share is falling. In 1995-98, the researchers estimate, ODA accounted for 82% of aid flows, private philanthropy for 17% and the new development partners for just 1%. A decade later, in 2005-08, they estimated that private philanthropy's share had almost doubled to 34% while the new development partners' share was up fivefold to 5%.

It's worth remembering, also, that aid is only one source of funds that can help countries' economies to develop. For example, investment by private firms may have profit as its primary motive, and is not classed as aid, but it can create jobs and contribute to a developing a country's industrial infrastructure. Equally, within developing countries, improving taxation systems can allow governments to spend more on education, healthcare and infrastructure (*see Chapter 7*).

Who provides aid?

Most people have heard of NGOs – non-governmental organisations – which encompass everything from religious charities to grassroots human-rights groups. But what about a Quango? That stands for quasi-autonomous NGO, according to a classification from Dutch researcher Sara Kinsbergen. Her list goes further: there is the Bongo, or business-organised NGO; the Engo, or environmental NGO; the Ingo, or international NGO; and, of course, the Gongo, or government-organised NGO – an apparent oxymoron, the term is occasionally used to describe an NGO set up by a government to take advantage of privileges or funding available to true NGOs. Last, and not least, there's the Mongo, or "my own NGO", a charity set up by an individual.

This list may be a little tongue in cheek, but it helps to make a serious point: the development world is complex, and becoming more so by the year. As well as traditional donor governments, like those of the DAC, there are emerging donors, like China and India, which are becoming important players. In addition, there are also government-supported aid agencies, multilateral organisations like the UN, development banks, any number of NGOs, and much, much more. Listing even a fraction of these would eat up much of the rest of the book. But it is useful to take a broad look at who does what.

Governments

The members of the OECD's DAC provide the bulk of the world's aid, but they are not the only government sources. A number of non-DAC members are also significant donors, for example Turkey, which gave $967 million in ODA in 2010. In recent years, there's also been a growing focus on the role of the emerging economies, especially the BRICS (Brazil, Russia, India, China and South Africa), most of which are themselves also aid recipients *(see Chapter 8)*. Their precise role is difficult to quantify, partly because – unlike DAC members – they don't routinely report data to an international agency and partly because they don't always have an official definition of what counts as aid. Nevertheless, some numbers are available: for example, Brazilian officials estimated their aid activities were worth $362 million in 2009, while China's aid in the same year was estimated (but not confirmed) at $1.9 billion by Chinese research institutions. According to official data from China's government, the cumulative total of the country's foreign aid stood at just over 256 billion yuan (about $39 billion) by 2009. Most of it was bilateral and about four-fifths of it went to Asia and Africa. Like many traditional donors, the new development partners engage with other developing countries at a number of different levels, including technical co-operation. India, for instance, has provided training and education in areas like environmental management and IT to 40 000 people in other developing countries through the Indian Technical and Economic Co-operation programme.

Multilateral donors

As we've seen, a large slice of aid – around 40% – is channelled through an estimated 200 multilateral donors and agencies, such as The World Bank and United Nations. Multilaterals are "owned" by their member governments – some are regional, such as the European Union's agencies, while others are truly international, such as the United Nations, which has more than 190 member governments. In aid terms, multilaterals fall into four main categories:

Development banks: The best-known internationally is The World Bank, but there are also a number of regional agencies, such as the African and the Asian Development Banks. All focus mainly on lending to developing countries, but they are also a source of expertise and advice. Confusingly, The World Bank is itself made up of two separate institutions: The International Bank for Reconstruction and Development (IBRD), which focuses on middle-income countries and the stronger lower-income countries, and the International Development Association (IDA), which deals only with the world's poorest countries. The World Bank Group also includes a number of other agencies, such as the International Finance Corporation (IFC), which offers financing, guarantees and advice to privately-owned enterprises in developing countries.

United Nations: The UN is active in many areas of development – indeed, it says of itself that the issue consumes "the vast majority of the Organization's resources". UN efforts range from providing emergency and humanitarian assistance through agencies like the World Food Programme, to pursuing longer-term development goals, like poverty reduction and strengthening governance.

Europe: The combined efforts of the 27 members of the European Union make it collectively the world's largest donor. Although there is a high degree of co-operation among EU Member States, much of their aid effort still reflects the development priorities of individual countries.

Global funds: Over the past decade or so, a number of special agencies have been set up to pursue particular development goals, the best known being the Global Fund to Fight AIDS, Tuberculosis and Malaria, which was created in 2002. Unlike UN agencies such as the World Health Organization, the Global Fund is solely a financing agency.

Multilateral donors have many advantages in development. By pooling funds from multiple donors, they can cut the cost of administration, and save recipients the trouble of liaising with numerous individual donors. Their neutrality can also allow them to provide political "cover" for national governments with contentious aid decisions. And, unlike national governments, they can often have a more global vision, giving them a stronger hand in tackling international issues like climate change.

Against that, multilaterals have sometimes suffered from a perception that they're bureaucratic and expensive; that they lack transparency and are too remote from the people they're supposed to be helping. And even some of the advantages of multilaterals, such as the pooling of resources, can pose a problem for donors. That's because in order to maintain support for aid programmes with domestic voters, donor governments usually want to show that aid money is having an impact. But when money is poured into a multilateral, that can be hard to do. That's part of the reason why donors often "earmark" their funding to multilaterals. It may also be behind the fall in general funding for UN agencies in recent years, and its replacement by funding for specific UN programmes and, especially, the global funds.

> "... as the aid given to a multilateral is pooled before being allocated to partner countries, this makes individual donors less visible and gives them less control over specific aid destinations."
>
> Emily Bosch, *OECD Journal: General Papers*

Non-governmental organisations

NGOs (also referred to as civil society organisations, or CSOs) have become increasingly active in development in recent decades, in both developed and developing countries. Some are mostly national, like the Irish aid charity Concern, and others are international, like Oxfam. NGOs are important sources of development funding in their own right: according to OECD estimates in 2009, NGOs in developed countries raise between $20 billion and $25 billion a year in private contributions to development assistance. Governments also use them as a channel for official aid: about 10% of ODA goes to NGOs, rising to as much as a quarter of ODA in the United States. There are also growing numbers of NGOs in developing countries, such as the Kenya-based Green Belt Movement, created by the late Nobel laureate Wangari Maathai, which campaigns on environmental issues and supports this with practical action like tree-planting. Governments in developing countries also use NGOs to deliver services on the ground: in the 1990s, for example, India's government quadrupled the amount of money it allocated to NGOs.

The role of NGOs has come to be increasingly recognised in development, especially their power to represent the voice of communities and social groups, such as women, that have in the past been excluded from the development debate. But their proliferation has also contributed to the growing complexity of the development world, making it ever more difficult to co-ordinate aid and development co-operation and avoid unnecessary and wasteful overlaps.

"CSOs are … often particularly effective at reaching the poor and socially excluded, providing humanitarian assistance, mobilising community efforts, speaking up for human rights and gender equality, and helping to empower particular constituencies."
Civil Society and Aid Effectiveness (2009)

Private philanthropy

It's a remarkable reflection on the scale of his donations that Bill Gates is now perhaps better known as a philanthropist than as the man who gave the world Microsoft Windows. In the 16 years since it was founded in 1994, the Gates Foundation has committed more than $24 billion in grants for global health and development. In 2009, it contributed $1.8 billion in health aid alone, making it the world's third largest such contributor to this sector, exceeded only by the United States and The Global Fund.

The Gates Foundation is unusual in the scale of its donations. What's less unusual about it is that it's American: by a large margin, the bulk of the world's private philanthropy comes from the United States. In part, that's a reflection of the scale of America's economy, a tax system that provides strong incentives for giving to charity, and a long tradition that sees it as noble to give charity. For many people, the example was set by Andrew Carnegie, a self-made Scottish-American businessman who gave up working at the age of 65 and devoted the rest of his life to giving away his fortune in order to avoid what he described as the "disgrace" of dying rich. Critics, however, suggest that the scale of American philanthropy is a reflection of enormous wealth inequalities – too many rich people with too much money on their hands – and inadequate government welfare provision.

Private philanthropy takes many different forms: diaspora groups – typically emigrants and their descendents – are one source, as are religious groups, representing most of the world's main faiths, including Buddhism, Christianity, Islam, and Judaism. A substantial amount comes from foundations, some of which are associated with individuals, like the Mo Ibrahim Foundation, which works to raise standards of governance in Africa, and others with businesses or wealthy families. Mo Ibrahim is part of a trend that has seen a big rise in the number of foundations in North America and the European Union, as successful entrepreneurs follow the examples of billionaires like Bill Gates and Warren Buffet. This has also spread to developing countries themselves, with the emergence of donors like telecoms tycoon Carlos Slim in Mexico and property developer Huang Rulun in China.

Many businesses also provide aid, sometimes as a cash donation and sometimes "in kind", which can include acts like providing expertise, scholarships or discounts on goods sold to developing countries. In June 2011, a number of Western drug companies announced big cuts in the price they charge for the rotavirus vaccine, which protects against a major cause of diarrhoea, in developing countries. Typically, the vaccine costs $50 per shot in a developed country, but this will fall to as little as $2.50 in poor countries. No area of aid is exempt from controversy, and private philanthropy is no exception: critics say that, unlike governments, private philanthropists are answerable to no one and, in some cases, they may use aid to further their business interests.

What does it all add up to?

This chapter has explored some of the complexities of the development world, including the major actors and their respective roles. But even a brief glance at all this effort and activity raises an inevitable question: what does it all achieve? That will be the subject of the next chapters. Before that, however, and over the next few pages, we'll look at where ODA comes from, where it goes, and the ways in which it can be measured.

3. What is aid?

Aid – some numbers

This section introduces some basic numbers on who gives and gets official development assistance, or ODA, which is the world's largest single form of aid. Such aid can be measured from two different country perspectives – the donor's or the recipient's, and the total sums involved may differ depending on which perspective you choose.

Why? The reasons are often technical, and so beyond the scope of this book. But, to give a relatively simple example, take the case of loans from a multilateral agency like The World Bank. In general, if a donor country is channelling funds through The World Bank, it does so by giving a grant, which means the donor country expects never to see the money again. At that stage, The World Bank can take the money and use it to subsidise the interest on a much larger loan to a developing country borrower. So, from the perspective of the donor country, the money is a grant; but from the perspective of the recipient, it's part of a loan with interest payments that will be reflected on the balance sheet for as long as the loan is outstanding.

From both the donor and recipient perspective, aid volumes can be presented in a number of ways:

Donor perspective: From this angle, aid is typically measured either in absolute terms (how many millions or billions of dollars) or as a percentage of the donor country's GNI (*see box in Chapter 2*).

Recipient perspective: From this angle, aid is typically measured in three ways: the total amount received in dollars; the total as a percentage of the recipient country's GNI or GDP; and the amount received on average per person (or per capita) in the recipient country.

These different measures can be instructive, as illustrated by the example of two African countries: in 2009, Burkina Faso received $1.084 billion in ODA, while South Africa received $1.075 billion – roughly the same. But measure the ODA against the size of their economies, and the difference is much greater. For Burkina Faso, its ODA receipts were equivalent to 13.5% of GNI; for South Africa – a much wealthier country – they were equivalent to just under 0.4% of GNI.

3. What is aid?

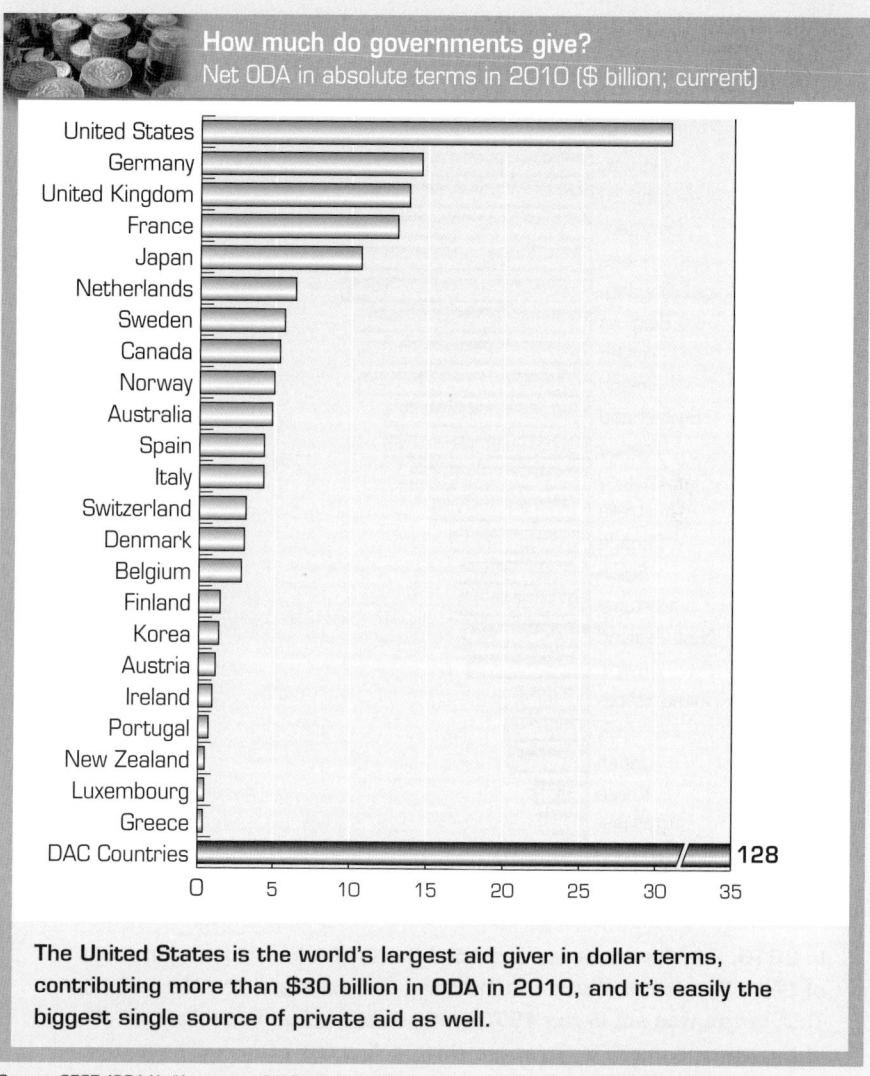

How much do governments give?
Net ODA in absolute terms in 2010 ($ billion; current)

The United States is the world's largest aid giver in dollar terms, contributing more than $30 billion in ODA in 2010, and it's easily the biggest single source of private aid as well.

Source: OECD (2011), "Aggregate Aid Statistics: ODA by donor", *OECD International Development Statistics* (database).

StatLink: http://dx.doi.org/10.1787/888932606207

3. What is aid?

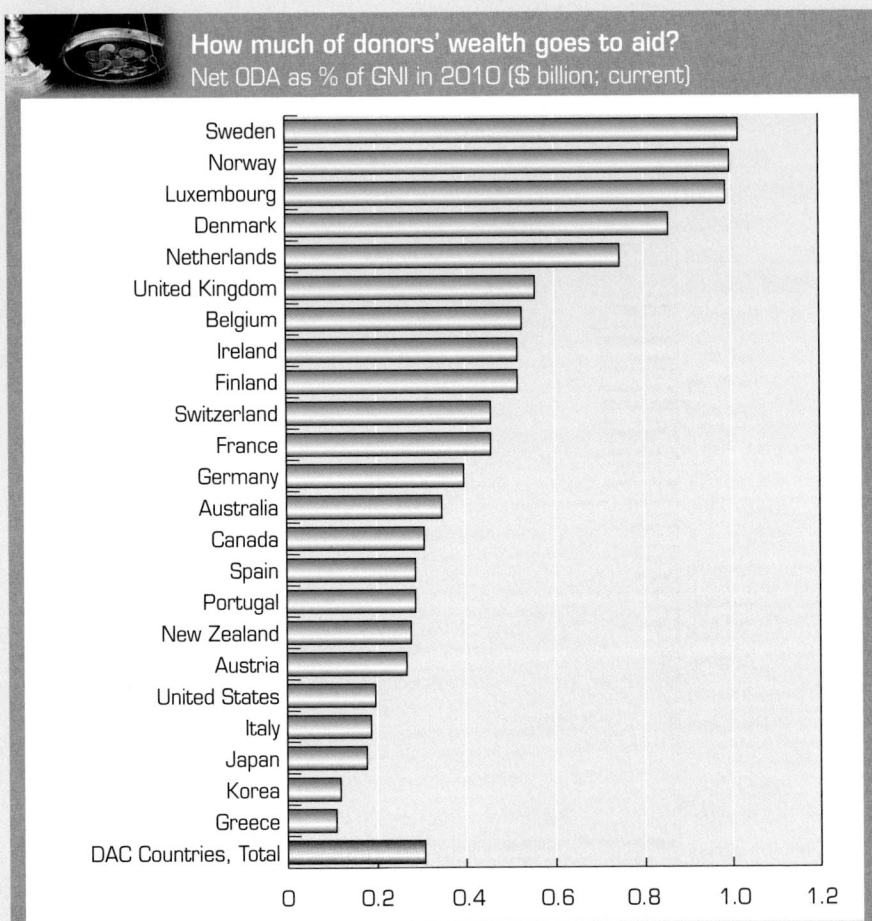

How much of donors' wealth goes to aid?
Net ODA as % of GNI in 2010 ($ billion; current)

In 2010, just five countries exceeded the target for aid giving of 0.7% of GNI – Sweden, Norway, Luxembourg, Denmark and The Netherlands. That target was set in the 1970s and accepted by most – but not all – of the major donors; in the years since only a few countries have ever attained it. In 2010, the DAC members as a group contributed 0.32% of GNI in aid, which matched the figure for 2005 and was the highest level since 1992.

Source: OECD (2011), "Aggregate Aid Statistics: ODA by donor", *OECD International Development Statistics* (database).
StatLink ⟶ : http://dx.doi.org/10.1787/888932606226

3. What is aid?

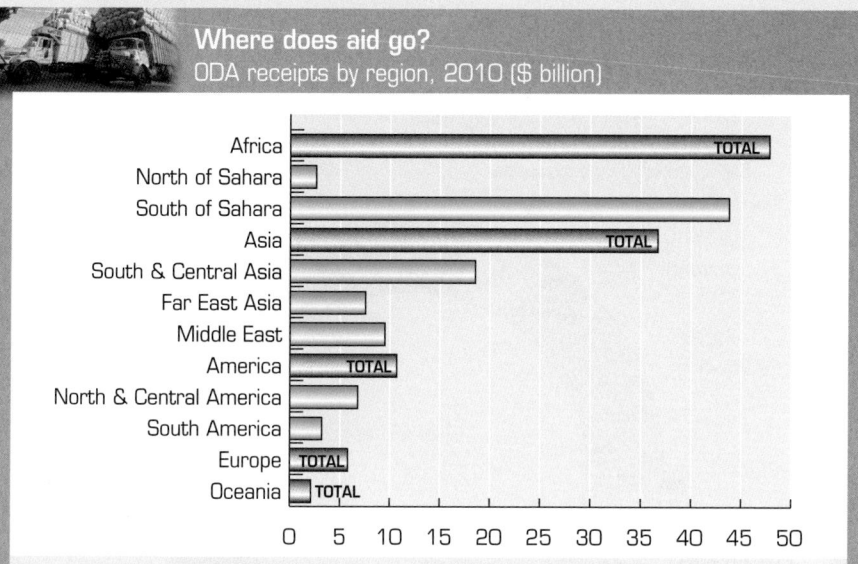

Where does aid go?
ODA receipts by region, 2010 ($ billion)

Sub-Saharan Africa is the largest recipient of aid, and the amount has tended to rise in recent years. In 2005, the region received just over $32 billion in aid; by 2010, the figure stood at almost $44 billion. By contrast, total aid to Asia – which includes the Middle East – fell substantially, from more than $46.5 billion to around $36.7 billion. Much of the decline was due to a big drop in aid to Iraq: its aid receipts stood at over $22 billion in 2005, due to exceptional debt relief that year, but fell to $2.2 billion in 2010.

Source: OECD (2011), "Aggregate Aid Statistics: ODA by recipient by country", *OECD International Development Statistics* (database).

StatLink : http://dx.doi.org/10.1787/888932606245

3. What is aid?

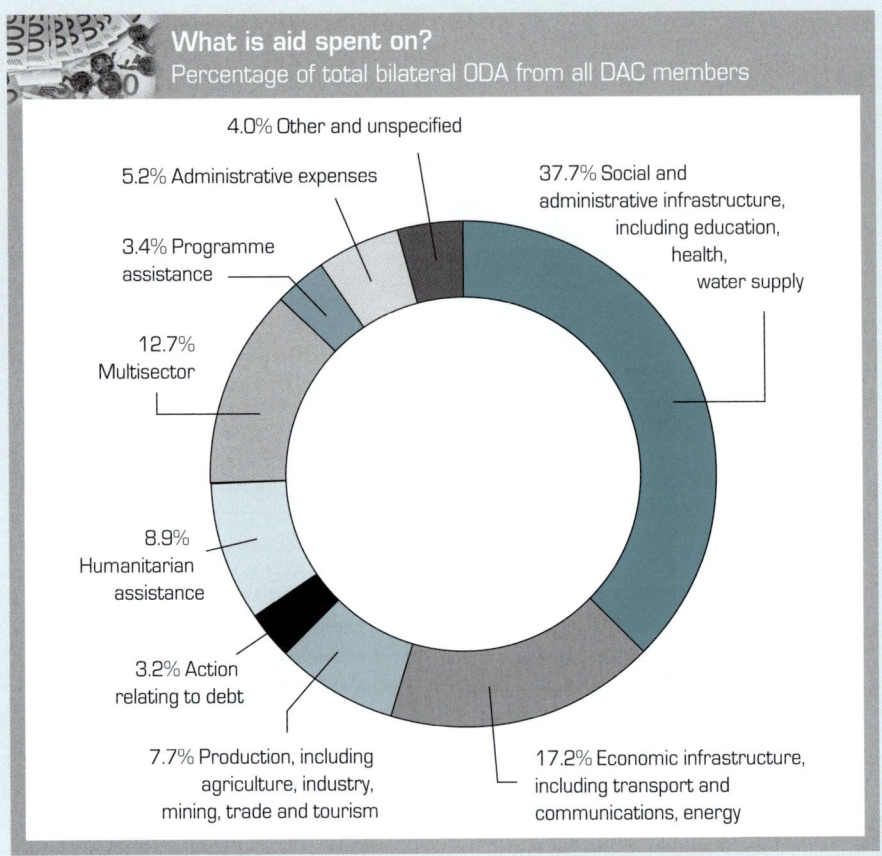

Source: Development Co-operation Report 2011.

StatLink: http://dx.doi.org/10.1787/888932606264

Find Out More

FROM OECD ...

On the Internet

Aid data can be accessed at **Aidflows** (*www.aidflows.org*), an interactive website created by the OECD, The World Bank and the Asian Development Bank.

To access the full range of **aid data and statistics** from the OECD's Development Assistance Committee, go to *www.oecd.org/dac/stats*. The **DAC databases** cover bilateral and multilateral donors' aid and other resource flows to developing countries in two separate databases:

▶ The **DAC annual aggregates database** provides comprehensive data on the volume, origin and types of aid and other resource flows.

▶ The **Creditor Reporting System** provides detailed information on individual aid activities, such as sectors, countries and project descriptions.

Data can be accessed at the user-friendly **QWIDS** website (*http://stats.oecd.org/qwids*); more advanced users may prefer to use the **OECD's dot.stat** portal (*http://stats.oecd.org*).

A **glossary of key terms and concepts** in development co-operation can be found at *www.oecd.org/dac/glossary*.

Publications

Development Co-operation Report (series): Published annually, this report is the flagship publication of the OECD's Development Assistance Committee. It's a source of commentary and analysis on key topics in development co-operation and aid effectiveness, and provides an annual summary of the latest data on DAC members' aid activities.

... AND OTHER SOURCES

Does Foreign Aid Really Work, by Roger C. Riddell (Oxford, 2007): An in-depth examination of development co-operation by a British aid specialist. It discusses the history of aid, provides detailed explanations of much of the key terminology and assesses the impact of aid.

A Primer on Foreign Aid (*www.cgdev.org/files/8846_file_WP92.pdf*): This short primer by Steven Radelet of the Centre for Global Development provides a brief and accessible introduction to many of the key terms and ideas in development assistance.

Centre for Global Development (*www.cgd.org*): This US-based group aims to provide, in its own words, "independent research and practical ideas for global prosperity". It conducts research on a wide range of policy areas that can potentially affect the prospects of developing countries. Research areas include aid effectiveness, globalisation, education, health, trade and migration.

One (*www.one.org*): Co-founded by Irish rock star Bono, One describes itself as a "non-partisan ... advocacy and campaigning organization that fights extreme poverty and preventable disease". It monitors aid commitments by leading donors, including those on the DAC, with a special focus on support for Africa.

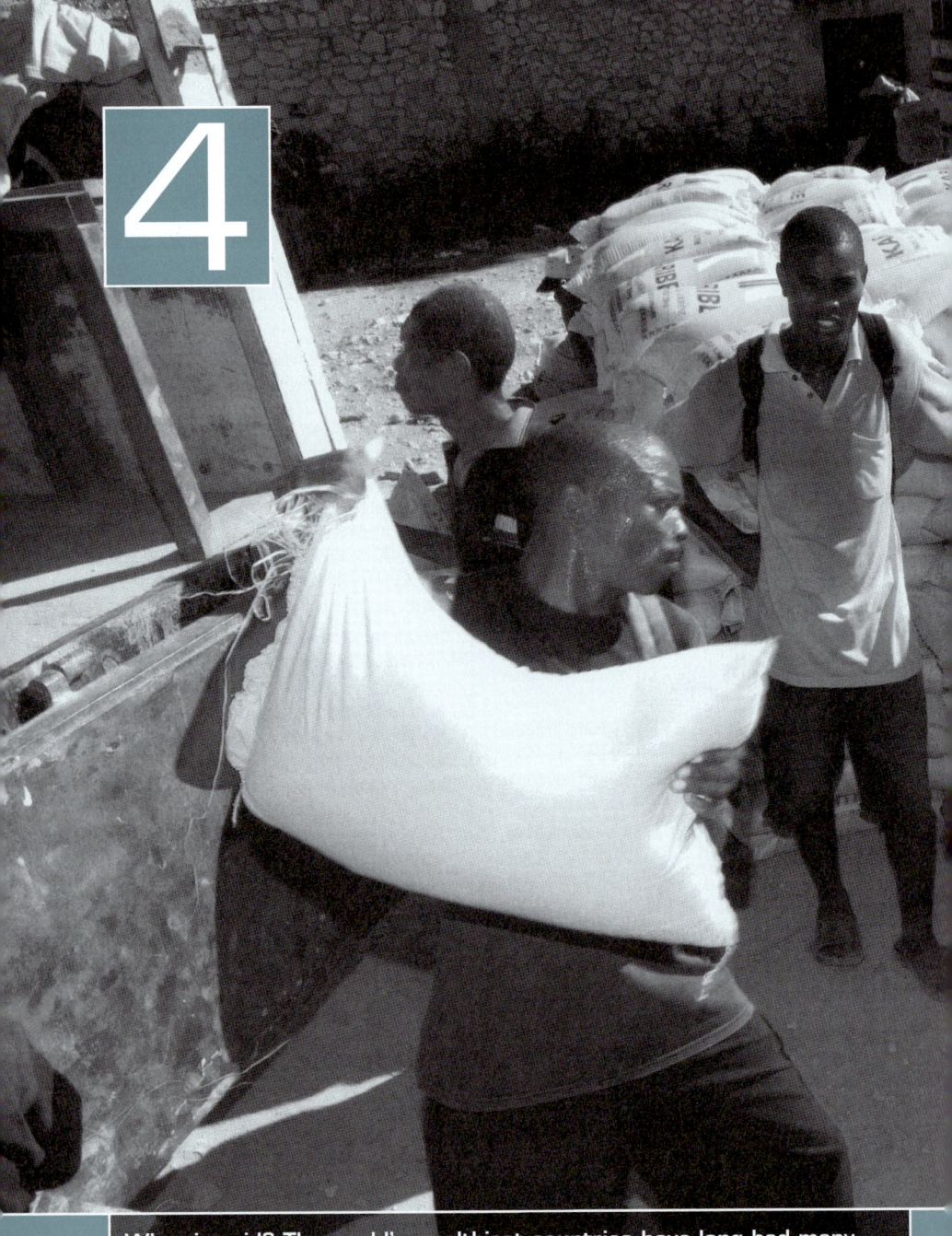

4

Why give aid? The world's wealthiest countries have long had many reasons for working with developing countries, from alleviating hardship to exercising influence. In recent years, other factors have moved up the agenda, not the least of which is a desire to strengthen global security.

Shifting development goals and motivations

4. Shifting development goals and motivations

By way of introduction ...

In 1949, US President Harry S. Truman was inaugurated for his second term. It was less than four years since his first inauguration following the death in office of President Franklin D. Roosevelt, and the world Truman was facing was a very different place. World War II was over, but many of the combatants, especially in Europe, were still struggling to get back on their feet. The divisions of the Cold War were already in place, and would only deepen in the years to come.

It was against this backdrop that on 20 January, Truman gave his inaugural address. Not surprisingly much of his speech focused on foreign affairs, and he made four main points. The first three mostly represented the continuation of past policies, but the fourth set down a new challenge: " ... We must embark on a bold new programme for making the benefits of our scientific advances and industrial progress available for the improvement and growth of underdeveloped areas," Truman declared. He justified his commitment to development co-operation in this way: "More than half the people of the world are living in conditions approaching misery. ... Their poverty is a handicap and threat both to them and to more prosperous areas."

Flash forward sixty years to early 2009, and another US President is talking about development. After announcing plans to send an extra 17 000 troops to Afghanistan, Barack Obama tells a reporter that defence policy is only one part of his strategy to stabilise the troubled region: "I am absolutely convinced that you cannot solve the problem of Afghanistan, the Taliban, the spread of extremism in the region solely through military means. ... We're going to have to use diplomacy. We're going to have to use development."

▶ Although separated by six decades, the links between Truman's "Four Point" speech and Obama's "3D" foreign policy are striking. Both make an explicit connection between development and security, saying, in effect, that while development is a desirable goal in its own right, it's also crucial to ensuring the safety of the international community. But security issues are only a part of what motivates development co-operation: philanthropy and moral purpose, historical and cultural ties between countries, trading relationships and so on also matter. Equally, the goals of development co-operation – from seeking to help lay the foundations for economic growth to improving basic living conditions – are varied, and have evolved over time. In this chapter, we'll look at how development co-operation has evolved since the 1960s, and use it as a lens to explore both the motivations and goals of donor governments.

Development co-operation: A brief history

The beginning of what might be called the aid era is often dated to Truman's inaugural address, which has been described by British aid scholar Roger Riddell as "the first speech by a national political leader outlining why and how it was necessary for governments to provide aid for the development of poor countries". But, as Riddell also points out, it's misleading to think that aid began on 20 January 1949. In reality, the idea had been around for quite some time. As far back as 1812, US legislators had authorised the president to purchase $50 000 worth of goods for Venezuela following an earthquake there. Other countries, too, had provided emergency assistance over the years and even longer-term development assistance, albeit mainly to their own overseas possessions. In 1929, the United Kingdom passed a Colonial Development Act to provide loans and grants for building infrastructure in the colonies. Its politicians were not shy in justifying such efforts as being in Britain's interests: speaking in the 1940s, a minister declared that "by one means or another, by hook or by crook, the development of primary production of all sorts in the colonial area … is … a life and death matter for the economy of the country". By country, he meant his own, the United Kingdom.

Four years after the catastrophe of the Second World War, Truman's 1949 speech came at a time when the world was in the mood for some optimism and the creation of a new international order. It's significant that many of today's institutions of global governance – the United Nations, The World Bank, the International Monetary Fund – date from the mid-to-late 1940s, as do statements of humanitarian intent like the Universal Declaration of Human Rights.

Truman was also speaking at a moment when the potential of development assistance and investment was being given very concrete expression in Europe. There, the Marshall Plan, a US-led reconstruction programme, was helping to rebuild countries ravaged by war. Between April 1948 and June 1951, Western Europe received about $13 billion from the United States for post-war reconstruction, equivalent to around $108 billion in 2006 dollars.

At the time of its operation, the plan was mostly warmly regarded: Britain's wartime prime minister Winston Churchill called it "the most unsordid act in history", while a foreign secretary, Ernest Bevin, said it was an act of "generosity … beyond belief". But there was also resistance. Speaking in the context of how aid is sometimes perceived in recipient countries, the historian Gérard Bossuat has noted that "many Europeans who were not anti-American resented the deep dependence of Europe vis-à-vis the United States".

Still, even today, more than 60 years after it ended, the Marshall Plan is often invoked when there's a call to arms for massive intervention in a social or economic crisis. And, in at least a couple of ways, it continues to make its impact felt in the area of development assistance. Firstly, it gave – and continues to give – an example of how large-scale assistance can make a difference: " … if aid worked in Europe, if it gave to Europe what Europe needed, why couldn't it do the same everywhere else?", the economist and aid critic Dambisa Moyo has written.

> "Today the Marshall Plan is now used to warn public opinion against an impending, unusually disastrous situation demanding immediate solution."
>
> Gérard Bossuat, *The Marshall Plan: History and Legacy*

Secondly, the body that managed the Marshall Plan in Europe, the Organisation for European Economic Co-operation (OEEC), would morph in the early 1960s into the Organisation for Economic Co-operation and Development (OECD) – a grouping of developed countries that, as its name suggests, was also profoundly concerned with the needs of developing countries. Established very early on under the OECD's umbrella were two bodies devoted entirely to development issues, the Development Assistance Committee (DAC) and the OECD Development Centre, both of which continue their work today (*see Chapter 1*).

The 1950s and 1960s coincided with a time of enormous political change in Africa and parts of Asia, as the last remnants of Europe's colonial empires began to be wound up. In 10 years up to the mid-1960s, more than 30 countries in Africa, and another handful in Southeast Asia, gained independence. The challenges facing these new countries, especially those in Africa, were great. Some were countries in name only, creations of the great European colonial carve-up rather than traditional nation states. In Africa particularly, many also suffered the geographical disadvantage of being landlocked. And while some were gifted with natural resources like oil and diamonds, they would go on to discover that these blessings could also be a curse. Finally, many had only minimal infrastructure, like roads and bridges, and very limited capacity to create power or supply treated water.

Working to get these new states – and other developing countries – on to firm foundations was a moral imperative. There were political calculations, too, which would only deepen as the rival Cold War blocs sought to win and retain allies in subsequent decades. And, as we've seen, the Marshall Plan served as a solid and recent example of how effective aid could be in getting broken countries back on their feet.

How much aid should countries give? As far back as 1958, the World Council of Churches had proposed that 1% of donor countries' wealth should go to developing countries. But it didn't distinguish between how much of that should come from government and how much from private donors. Fearful of big variations in private donations, developing countries wanted a concrete target to be set for official aid, and proposed a number: 0.75% of gross national income, or GNI *(see Chapter 2)*. At the end of the 1960s, that idea was endorsed by the Pearson Commission, the first international commission on international development, although it went for a slightly lower number, 0.7% of GNI. In 1970 this became the agreed target among most – but not all – of the major donors, although in the years since, only a few developed-world countries have ever reached it, and then for only very short periods.

4. Shifting development goals and motivations

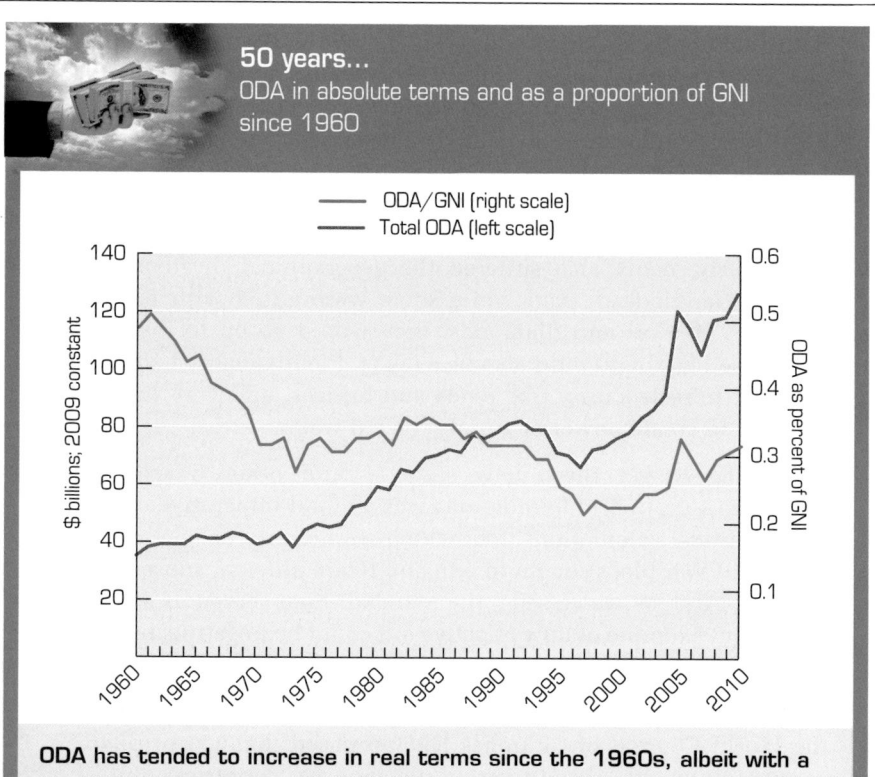

50 years...
ODA in absolute terms and as a proportion of GNI since 1960

ODA has tended to increase in real terms since the 1960s, albeit with a few dips, such as in the mid-1990s when donor countries went through a period of post-recession fiscal consolidation. By 2010, it reached a new high – in real terms – of $128.7 billion. By contrast, the trajectory of ODA as a percentage of GNI (a measure of donors' national wealth) has been rather less clear. It fell throughout the 1960s, oscillated up and down throughout the 1970s and 1980s and fell again throughout much of the 1990s before picking up in the early 2000s.

Source: Development Co-operation Report 2011.
StatLink: http://dx.doi.org/10.1787/888932606283

Gathering clouds – the 1970s and 1980s

The 1950s and 1960s have been described as the "glory years" for development assistance. But as the 1970s dawned, some of the initial enthusiasm and optimism had begun to fade. That mood would deepen – with various ups and downs – over the next couple of decades, especially in the case of Africa: "The colonial legacy atrophied as it was bound to do and authentic local systems took a long time to put in place," says Richard Manning, a former chairman of the OECD's Development Assistance Committee. "The '70s and '80s were pretty dire. It got worse rather than better … countries got very economically out of balance." In developed countries, too, the 1970s proved gloomy, with the oil shock of 1973 effectively bringing down the curtain on the almost three decades of relatively strong growth that followed the Second World War in many OECD countries.

Against this background of economic turbulence and contraction, the focus began to shift. Throughout the 1960s, aid had been targeted mainly at infrastructure development in the belief that this would provide momentum for wider economic growth. But in the 1970s, the idea that economic growth would in and of itself be enough to lift all boats came to be questioned. Instead, aid came increasingly to be targeted at satisfying "basic human needs". This approach was grounded in the belief that economic growth alone could not guarantee that people would receive things like proper nutrition and education; satisfying those needs was rather a foundation on which to build growth.

The impact of the oil shocks continued to be felt in the 1980s. Throughout the 1970s, the major oil producers had seen a substantial rise in their revenues as oil prices rose. Much of that money went to banks in the West, which in turn lent it to developing countries, especially in South America. In the early 1980s, the real price of that borrowing began to be felt as countries struggled to make their repayments. In 1982, Mexico finally admitted it could not repay its loans, and defaulted on its debt, sparking a crisis that would eventually sweep through the continent. African countries, too, struggled increasingly with debt from the 1980s.

The debt crisis led to another major shift in approaches to development aid. Increasingly, donors began insisting that developing countries make substantial changes in their economic management. Two ideas came to dominate: **stabilisation** and **structural adjustment**. The first required developing countries to "stabilise" their economies, for example by reducing fiscal imbalances; the second called for fundamental structural reforms such as trade liberalisation. Aid came attached with ever more "conditionalities" and policy advice, which today are often criticised. The economist Jeffrey Sachs has characterised the donors' approach in this way: "The rich countries told the poor countries: 'Poverty is your own fault. Be like us (or what we imagine ourselves to be – free market-oriented, entrepreneurial, fiscally responsible) and you, too, can enjoy the riches of private-sector-led economic development'."

While it's true that many developing countries went through a period of what Sachs calls "profound economic mismanagement" in the 1980s, the prescriptions from Western countries for overcoming these problems are now widely seen as having gone too far. Certainly, they went well beyond what might have been needed to make aid *itself* more effective. Their aim instead was almost to impose an entire economic philosophy on developing countries, as Roger Riddell has noted: "In line with neo-liberal orthodoxies, recipients were 'encouraged' to open up their markets, privatise state assets, adopt a more export-oriented, less protective trade regime as a *quid pro quo* for receiving aid, and reduce direct government expenditures, a condition from which key services, such as health and education, were not to be exempted."

Another key trend in the 1980s was the growing – albeit sporadic – media spotlight on Africa and an ever-higher profile for non-government organisations, or NGOs. This wasn't an entirely new phenomenon: the famine in Biafra in 1969 had gained headlines worldwide and led to charity fund-raising events, while significant NGOs like Médecins Sans Frontières have been in place since the 1970s. But the process speeded up greatly in the 1980s, fuelled in part by high-profile events like the 1985 Live Aid concert to raise funds for famine victims in Ethiopia. This has continued right up to today, with NGOs attaining an ever-higher profile in development. On the positive side, this has bought an influx of fresh funds and ideas; less positively, it has added greatly to the complexity and bureaucracy of the development world.

After the Wall – 1990s and 2000s

The collapse of the Soviet bloc at the turn of the decade had important ramifications for the development world. At one level, some of the geopolitical motivations for development co-operation – the desire to keep developing countries on one side or the other of the East-West divide – were swept away. Partly as a result of this, real net ODA fell by nearly a third across the decade, having risen in real terms throughout much of the 1980s.

> " ... aid fell sharply after the end of the Cold War and of superpower rivalry in the Third World. By 1997, and in three of the subsequent four years, it was at an all-time low of 0.22% of donors' combined national income."
>
> *Development Co-operation Report 2003*

In Latin America and Asia, much of the loss was more than countered by a rise in private investment, but this wasn't always the case in Africa. Another impact of the fall of the Berlin Wall was a new focus on providing assistance for countries in Central and Eastern Europe as they struggled to cope with turbulent political and economic change. The needs of these regions were very real: in the former Soviet Union, for instance, the number of people living in poverty rose from just over 2 million in 1987-88 to just under 58 million in 1993-95. But this new challenge also served to push "traditional" development regions, like Africa and Latin America, down the international agenda.

The 1990s brought some new thinking on development, and a fresh focus on the need to put people at the centre of the picture. This was reflected in the creation of UNDP's influential *Human Development Report* and Index in 1990, which stated as their underlying philosophy that "people are the real wealth of a nation". It was also evident in The World Bank's *World Development Report* of that year, which took as its title a single, stark word – *Poverty*. While noting improvements in much of the developing world since the 1960s, the report stated pointedly that: "Against that background of achievement, it is all the more staggering – and all the more shameful – that more than one billion people in the developing world are living in poverty."

But if thinking began to change in the 1990s, so too did the atmosphere, and not for the better. By the middle of the decade, there was growing talk of "donor fatigue" and the emergence of a continuing critique that claims, in blunt terms, that aid doesn't work. In partial response, the global development community set out to fix firm targets for results, which could provide a real yardstick to show just how aid was – or wasn't – working. As we saw in Chapter 2, that process – in which the OECD played a major role with the publication of *Shaping the 21st Century* – led to the creation of the Millennium Development Goals, which set down a series of ambitious targets for development to be attained by the year 2015. The MDGs also embodied the shift in the 1990s towards thinking about development in terms of people's living standards and life prospects.

As the 1990s closed, the dawn of the new millennium brought a sharp new focus on development. That came about for several reasons: one was the success of the high-profile Jubilee campaign in drawing attention to the debt burdens carried by many developing countries. Another – perhaps more urgent – was the 11 September attacks on the United States in 2001. Those attacks made explicit the links between development and security, a point made at the time by the then-chairman of the DAC, Jean-Claude Faure: "The events of 11 September have strengthened the conviction that a world without violence, terrorism and conflict also means a world freed from exclusion, vulnerability and inequality, a world where opportunities exist for all." In the years since, there's been increasing recognition of the fact that among the many motivations for donors to support developing countries, self-interest is not the least important. Or, as President Barack Obama put it when he addressed the Millennium Development Goals Summit in September 2010, "let's put to rest the old myth that development is mere charity that does not serve our interests."

Those self-interests also underlined the need to ensure that donors' resources are used as effectively as possible (a focus that only intensified in the wake of the Great Recession). Recent years have seen a growing focus on **aid effectiveness** and on improving our understanding of the conditions that enable aid to work. Much of this thinking took concrete form in the Paris Declaration on Aid Effectiveness *(see Chapter 6)*, which was adopted in 2005. Increasingly, development assistance came to be seen not as assistance but co-operation – a partnership between donors and developing countries, but with the latter in the driving seat. As Rwanda's President Paul Kagame has written, "We appreciate support from the outside, but it should be support for what we intend to achieve ourselves. No one should pretend that they care about our nations more than we do; or assume that they know what is good for us better than we do ourselves."

Arguably, developing countries have never before had such a wide a range of choices when it comes to charting their own course. Many, especially those enjoying a revival in their economic fortunes, saw their funding options grow substantially in the first years of the new millennium. Funding from private sources, such as business investment, became more significant; there was also the rise of philanthropic bodies like the Gates Foundation, which has become a major presence in the development world. And this has been followed up with the emergence of new partners, like China and India (*see Chapter 8*). By contrast, the role of traditional aid donors has declined in relative terms – although it remains very significant – as "aid" has itself become a less important source of funding for development in much of the world, albeit with some important exceptions. This marks just how much has changed over the past 50 years of development co-operation.

What motivates aid-giving?

This very short survey illustrates some of the many and evolving motivations behind giving aid over the years. A recent report from the Brookings Institution boiled them down to these four main headings:

Philanthropy: Initially, this tended to be couched in terms of charity – "we do good to give, but we are not morally blameworthy if we fail to do so," as Brian Opeskin characterises it. Later, the idea of aid as a moral obligation, rather than an optional charitable act, began to dominate. In this context, as Opeskin argues, aid may reflect two moral drivers: Firstly, concern for the wellbeing of our fellow human beings, regardless of where they live; secondly, a concern for natural justice, sometimes to correct past wrongs, such as colonialism, or to ensure a fairer distribution of the earth's resources.

Compensation: Those latter themes could probably also be thought of as a form of "compensation", however this idea has implications that go beyond that. One of the most notable at the moment relates to climate change. People in developed countries have historically produced the bulk of the "greenhouse gases" that, it's predicted, will lead to greater climate instability in the decades to come. However, according to World Bank estimates, at least three-quarters of the cost of this change will be borne by people in developing countries. Low-lying Pacific nations like Tuvalu and Kiribati have already begun feeling the impact: early in the new millennium, the highest high tides began washing over roads as well as cropland, leaving some people with no choice but to try to move to higher land. "I really don't know where they will go," Ben Namakin, an environmentalist in Kiribati told *The New York Times*. "They may move further inland, but the more they do that, they will end up on somebody else's land or reach the ocean on the other side, as the islands are too narrow."

Overall, The World Bank estimates that even a rise of two degrees centigrade in global temperatures could lead to a permanent reduction of 4% to 5% in annual income per person in Africa and South Asia compared with minimal losses in developed countries. Aid, it can be argued, should help prepare developing countries for these economic and social shocks. Since early in the new millennium, a "complex architecture" of funding sources for climate change adaptation has emerged, as one OECD report puts it. Three special funds were established in 2001, and The World Bank has also established a fund; in addition, country-to-country initiatives have also been set up.

> "Climate change risks will need to be considered systematically in development planning at all levels in order to build in adaptation measures."
> *Integrating Climate Change Adaptation into Development Co-operation: Policy Guidance, August 2009*

Investment: Aid can also be thought of as an investment, in other words, donors give away money and other resources in the hope of bigger returns – both for themselves and for developing countries – in the years to come. This idea was reflected by the G20 grouping of developing and developed countries in its 2010 Seoul

Development Consensus for Shared Growth. It stated that the "rest of the global economy, in its quest for diversifying the sources of global demand and destinations for investing surpluses, needs developing countries and [low-income countries] to become new poles of global growth". Such investments can take many forms, for instance supporting the development of market economies could be seen as a way of expanding the range of future trading partners. Investing in healthcare could improve the foundations of a developing country's human capital, while also reducing the risk of dangerous pandemics across the planet.

Aid can also be thought of as an investment in **security**. Even in Truman's time, this was an important item on the foreign policy agenda. But, as we've seen, it has become an even bigger issue since the 11 September 2001 attacks, a reality reflected in the increasing focus of development efforts on fragile states (*see Chapter 7*), and in policy approaches like the "3D" troika of defence, diplomacy and development espoused by more recent US administrations. But security is not simply an absence of conflict. Going back to 1994, the *Human Development Report* defined human security as "freedom from fear and freedom from want". As New Zealand's Prime Minister (1999-2008) Helen Clark states, "This radical shift away from traditional thinking on peace and the prevention of conflict argued, in essence, that security lies in development, not in arms." In a sense, then, achieving security can be thought of as a form of development.

Geographical influence: Finally, aid can also be a way for countries to wield influence and to acquire or retain access to natural resources. This was especially apparent during the Cold War era, when the Western bloc, led by Washington, and the Soviet bloc, led by Moscow, competed for allies in Africa, Southeast Asia and Latin America. The mood of the time was expressed by then-US President Richard Nixon, who once declared that "the main purpose of American aid is not to help other nations but to help ourselves". Aid decisions can also be motivated by historical links between countries, especially between former colonial powers and their old dependencies. To some extent, these may be driven by a wish to continue exercising influence, but they can also reflect a very complex mix of historical, social, linguistic and cultural ties which can prove difficult to undo in response to changing aid needs. As the DAC remarked of one its members, France, "While the heritage of the past is an advantage, its imprint continues to mark the entire co-operation system, to a certain extent making it difficult to manipulate." France is certainly not alone.

Understanding all these motivations is important: they can help to explain apparent inconsistencies in donors' aid decisions, especially in aid that goes from government to government (i.e. bilaterally) rather than via a large multilateral body like the United Nations. For example, most people in the aid world feel that individual donors should focus their aid on a small number of countries rather than fragmenting it across many recipients. This would simplify administration, allowing developing countries to spend less time liaising with donors. However, despite improvements, donors continue to spread their aid quite widely, in part, perhaps, because they wish to go on exercising influence in as many recipient countries as possible. Another example is the extent to which aid decisions are motivated by factors that are specific to donors, rather than the real needs of recipients. One 2009 OECD study suggested that "almost half of the predicted value of aid is determined by donor-specific factors, one-third by needs, a sixth by self-interest and only 2% by performance."

What are aid's objectives?

As our look at the history of aid shows, donors' objectives – which aren't always easy to disentangle from their motivations – have also evolved, with the focus shifting from strengthening infrastructure, to fulfilling "basic needs", to economic restructuring, and so on. A critic might accuse donors of inconsistency, and there might be some truth in that. But, against that, the issues facing both developing and developed countries in the 1960s are not the same as those of today. Approaches have had to evolve, in part, because the challenges themselves have evolved. Equally, both developing and developed countries have tried to learn from the mistakes of the past, which has led to changes in strategies.

Broadly speaking, the objectives of most aid can be placed into one or more of the following four categories, which are based on work by Steven Radelet of the Centre for Global Development:

Stimulating economic growth: This was an early focus of development aid and, although new priorities emerged later, it remains important. It's mostly achieved through investment in infrastructure, such as roads and bridges, spending on sectors like agriculture, manufacturing and mining, and encouraging innovation and technology sharing.

Supporting health, education and political systems: Aid is often targeted at providing better healthcare and education or at fulfilling environmental goals, such as encouraging sustainable agriculture. It can also work to support political systems, especially in states with weak governance. In Zambia, for example, the National Assembly has worked with a team of donors, including NGOs, to find ways of bringing parliament closer to the people. This has included building local constituency offices for legislators, so giving them a direct point of contact with their constituents. "We get at least twenty cases brought to us a day and sometimes people come in big groups. The office provides an opportunity for people to meet me without having to search for me at parliament or all over," Given Lubinda, a legislator in Lusaka, told Irish Aid. As we'll see in Chapter 6, strengthening systems of governance has become an increasing priority in development circles in recent years. Indirectly, such support can also ultimately build foundations for economic growth.

Providing emergency relief: Catastrophes – whether manmade or natural – can strike without warning, and disable the capacity of even developed countries to cope. Emergency relief can include the provision of food, clothing and shelter and emergency services, such as search-and-rescue and medical support.

Stabilising economies following an economic shock: Developing countries can be especially prone to what economists call "shocks," unexpected events that affect economic activity. The world experienced one of these in late 2008, when the financial crisis led to a short but sharp collapse in global trade. As a result, some developing countries saw prices for their exports collapse, greatly reducing earnings. In theory, aid can help cushion the blow. Does this actually happen? The evidence is mixed. To some extent, aid flows may be economically "pro-cyclical" – in other words, they tend to rise when economies are strengthening, and to fall when they are weakening. For example, in the wake of the recession of the early 1990s, aid from traditional donors fell sharply. However, there is also evidence to suggest that in the case of severe shocks, ramped-up aid has served as a partial buffer, especially to middle-income countries.

But does it all work?

So, the motivations and objectives for aid and development co-operation are complex, sometimes contradictory and continually evolving. But, when it comes down to it, the issue for most people is not about why aid is given but, simply, does it work? As we'll see in the next chapter, it does. But, as we'll also see, that's not to say it *always* works, or achieves as much as it could.

> Parts of this chapter are adapted from the *Development Co-operation Report 2011*.

Find Out More

FROM OECD ...

On the Internet

To download a **history** of the OECD's Development Assistance Committee – *The DAC: 50 Years, 50 Highlights* – go to www.oecd.org/dataoecd/22/26/47072129. pdf?contentId=47072130

To find out more about **how the DAC works**, download *Inside the DAC: A Guide to the OECD Development Assistance Committee* at www.oecd.org/dataoecd/43/32/40986871.pdf

... AND OTHER SOURCES

The development activities of individual DAC members are usually carried out by special agencies or the foreign affairs ministries. Find out more about each member's activities at the following links:

Australia: AusAid (*www.ausaid.gov.au*).

Austria: The Austrian Development Agency (*www.entwicklung.at/en/*).

Belgium: The Belgian Development Agency (*http://www.btcctb.org/*).

Canada: The Canadian International Development Agency (*www.acdi-cida.gc.ca*).

Denmark: Danida (*http://um.dk/en/danida-en/*).

European Union: Go to EUROPA.eu, and follow the links to "Development".

Finland: Ministry of Foreign Affairs (*http://formin.finland.fi*), and follow links to "Development Policy".

France: Le Groupe de l'Agence française de Développement (*www.afd.fr/home*).

Germany: Federal Ministry for Economic Cooperation and Development, BMZ (www.bmz.de); Deutsche Gesellschaft für Internationale Zusammenarbeit (GTZ) (*www.giz.de/en/*), a service company for development co-operation; and KfW, which covers development finance (*www.kfw.de*).

Greece: Ministry of Foreign Affairs (*www2.mfa.gr/www.mfa.gr/en-US*).

Ireland: Irish Aid (*www.irishaid.gov.ie/*).

Italy: Ministry of Foreign Affairs (*www.esteri.it/MAE/EN*).

Japan: Japan International Cooperation Agency (*www.jica.go.jp*) and Japan Bank for International Cooperation (*www.jbic.go.jp*).

Korea: Korean International Co-operation Agency (*www.koica.go.kr*).

Luxembourg: Lux-Development (*www.lux-development.lu*)

Netherlands: Ministry of Foreign Affairs (*www.minbuza.nl/en/Key_Topics/Development_Cooperation*).

New Zealand: NZAid (*www.aid.govt.nz*).

Norway: Norwegian Agency for Development Co-operation (*www.norad.no*).

Portugal: Portuguese Institute for Development Support (*www.ipad.mne.gov.pt*).

Spain: Spanish Agency for International Development (*www.aecid.es/es*).

Sweden: Swedish International Development Co-operation Agency (*www.sida.se*).

Switzerland: Swiss Agency for Development and Co-operation (*www.deza.admin.ch*).

United Kingdom: Department for International Development (*www.dfid.gov.uk*).

United States: United States Agency for International Development (*www.usaid.gov*) and Millennium Challenge Corporation (*www.mcc.gov*).

Note: For space reasons, this listing is not comprehensive; for more information go to *www.oecd.org/linklist/0,2678, en_2649_33721_1797105_1_1_1_1,00. html#46158859*

5

Does development co-operation get results? A simple question with a simple answer – Yes. Or, rather: Yes, but not always. The distinction is important: understanding what makes it work, and what holds it back, is essential to delivering maximum benefits.

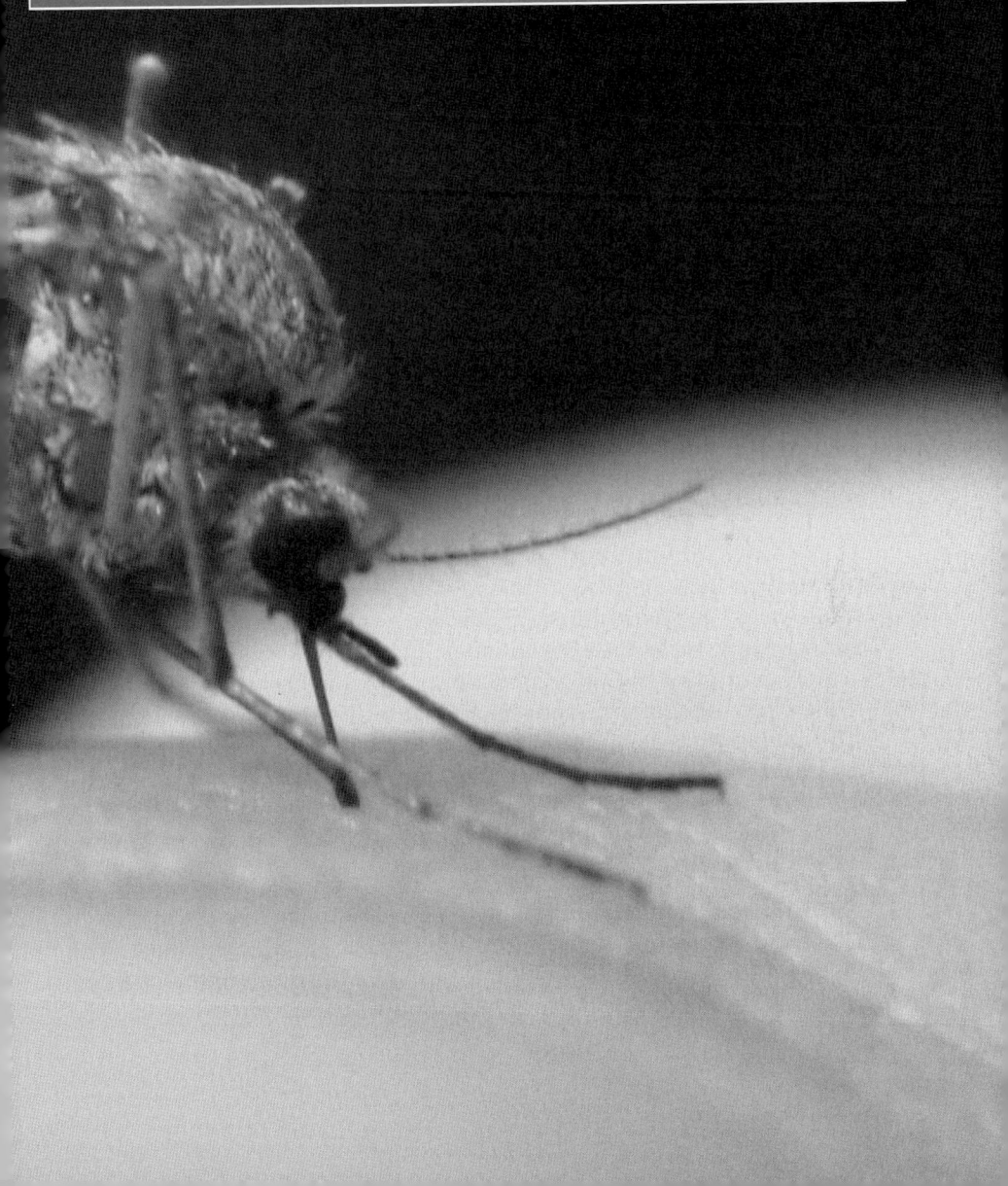

Are we getting results?

5. Are we getting results?

By way of introduction ...

If you live in a wealthy country, a mosquito is usually just an irritation – a whining pest that disturbs a summer evening. If you live in a developing country, a mosquito can be a killer. Every year, the insects infect millions of people with malaria, a disease that kills more than 700 000 people a year and claims the life of a child every 45 seconds in Africa. Malaria can be treated, but not cured, which is why the best treatment is prevention. That's not as hard as it sounds: over the past decade or so, there's been substantial progress in fighting malaria thanks in part to the distribution of insecticide-impregnated bed nets and to training people on how to prevent mosquitoes from breeding.

The benefits can be seen in Labangi, a village in one of India's poorest states, Orissa, where most families have lost someone to malaria. Health workers in the village are being trained in how to diagnose malaria and provide immediate treatment. That's important: treatment is most effective when it's delivered within a day of the victim first developing the high fever that's characteristic of the disease. They're also distributing bed nets, and helping to dispel misconceptions about them. "It was not easy to convince people to use bed nets," one health worker, Suhasini Behera, told the UK's Department for International Development (DFID). "People feared the nets were poisonous as there had been reports of rashes and itching from the insecticide."

The scale of the programme is impressive: in early 2010, 1.2 million bed nets were distributed to villagers in the state. In addition, 20 000 health workers have been trained in spotting and treating the disease. It's a big undertaking for the state government, which is running the programme. But it's being backed by DFID with a special grant of more than $150 million over five years. The campaign is having a real impact on people's lives: "Malaria was a huge problem in our area," Milu Jani, a local man whose father died from malaria, told DFID. "Now everyone in the village is using a net. I have lost my father but now I can keep my family safe from malaria."

Worldwide, more and more people are now safe from malaria thanks to a huge international push to combat the disease. Much of the effort has been led by the Roll Back Malaria Partnership, a UN- and World Bank-led grouping involving governments, non-governmental organisations (NGOs), development agencies, academics, and many others. The result has been greatly increased distribution of bed nets, diagnosis kits and medicines in affected areas, and a big fall in disease rates. In Africa in 2010, 11 countries halved the number of confirmed malaria cases or malaria admissions and deaths over the past decade. There was a similar fall in 32 of the 56 malaria-endemic countries outside Africa. What's happened? "The explanation for the turnaround is threefold," according to Margaret Chan, director-general of the World Health Organization (WHO). "The commitment of Africa's leaders, generous financial support from donor countries and institutions, and enlightened leadership and co-operation among the more than 500 partners that make up the Roll Back Malaria Partnership."

▶ Development co-operation works. Aid works. Successes like the campaign against malaria prove those propositions definitively. But do they *always* work? The answer to that is equally clear – No. Like anything else, development co-operation experiences successes and failures. How far do those successes outweigh the failures? This chapter – or, indeed, this book – is not long enough to answer that question definitively, but it will at least look at the debate that surrounds it, as well as at the concrete ways in which governments and agencies evaluate how well development initiatives are working.

What are the critiques of aid?

"Foreign aid in different times and different places has […] been highly effective, totally ineffective, and everything in between." Those words from The World Bank, one of the world's largest aid providers, sum up the vast range of experiences with aid over the decades. For every example of a situation or a country where it didn't work, it's usually possible to find an example of where it did.

This mixed record has generated intense debate over the impact of aid and development co-operation, with critiques typically coming from two main perspectives:

- ▶ The first is the big (or "macro"), picture: have development initiatives driven overall economic development and national prosperity?

5. Are we getting results?

> The second concerns their specific impact (or what's sometimes called the "micro" picture): have they helped raised health levels, allowed more children to go to school, and so on?

Those two perspectives deliver an enduring paradox: While development initiatives can be clearly shown to deliver specific benefits on the ground, the picture is much more mixed when it comes to their overall economic impact.

The big picture

When it comes to the overall economic impact of development co-operation, particularly in Africa, a typical criticism goes something like this: "ODA to sub-Saharan Africa from all sources since 1980 was equivalent to 146% of the region's 2008 GDP – seven times the equivalent Marshall Plan aid to the United Kingdom from 1946 to 1952," writes Brett Schaefer of the Heritage Foundation, a conservative American think tank. And yet, "despite ... vast investment, few recipients have achieved substantial improvements in per capita income. In fact, the record demonstrates that recipients of aid are just as likely to flounder economically as they are to prosper." In summary, there's been plenty of aid, and yet countries are still poor. Therefore, aid doesn't work.

Even the strongest advocates of aid would probably concede that the high hopes for economic development of the 1960s, particularly in Sub-Saharan Africa, have not been realised. But how much of that failure can be attributed to aid? Aid advocates argue that the problem has not been too much aid, but too little. Both sides of this debate could be argued over forever. But it might be more useful to step back and take a look at the wider contexts in which aid operates. Two aspects are especially worth noting: the relative size of aid in the economy of a developing country; and whether or not the policies of developed countries, and the rules of the global economy, are "development friendly".

Relative size of aid: For most developing countries, aid is relatively small in relation to the size of their total economies. In 2009 in Sub-Saharan Africa, for example, aid was equivalent to more than a tenth of total economic activity (as measured by GNI) in only 22 of 50 countries. Raise the bar to a fifth of GNI, and this number falls to just five countries. To give a sense of the range, in South Africa, aid was equivalent to slightly under 0.4% of GNI; at the other end of the scale, it was equivalent to just over 78% of GNI in Liberia. These figures are important, because they underline the reality that in most developing countries aid can really only be a catalyst for economic development. On its own, it simply isn't substantial enough to pull an up economy by its bootstraps. Should it be? Should massive amounts of aid be poured into poor countries to kick start development? Some would argue that it should; on the other hand, and as we'll see shortly, studies of the impact of aid suggest it can suffer from diminishing returns after a certain point. Recognising this dilemma, participants from developing and developed countries at the High-Level Forum on Aid Effectiveness in late 2011 in Busan, Korea, declared: "We will rethink what aid should be spent on and how, in ways that are consistent with agreed international rights, norms and standards, so that aid catalyses development."

Development-friendly policies: Aid flows are just one point of contact between developed and developing countries. There are many others, including trade, migration flows, investment and so on. All these exchanges can have an impact on the economic fate of developing countries: For example, much of the economic success of the Asian economies was built on trade, a good deal of which was with developed economies. The Asian economies benefited from a general relaxation of trade rules over the past few decades. But the policies of developed countries don't always work in favour of developing countries, and can even contradict the good intentions of official assistance. It's thus important from a development context that the policies of developed countries are coherent, and don't undermine aid goals. We'll look at this subject in greater detail in the next chapter.

Does aid promote growth?

When thinking about the role of aid in driving overall economic development, we need to see it within these contexts. In effect, if we think aid alone can end poverty, we're likely to be disappointed. So, keeping that in mind, let's go back to the original question – does aid promote growth? The evidence, as we've seen, is mixed, and can be interpreted in three ways according to Steven Radelet of the Centre for Global Development – "yes", "no" and "yes, but".

5. Are we getting results?

Yes, aid promotes growth (up to a point): In this, the most positive, scenario, aid is a bit like getting someone to push your stalled car on a cold morning. On your own, you can't move it, but with the help of a friend you can overcome your car's inertia and soon get rolling. Aid, arguably, can play a similar role: where poor countries lack the capital to finance investment, aid can give them a push and help build the foundations for subsequent, self-sustaining prosperity. Aid can also build "human capital" by strengthening education and health systems, which can ultimately fuel growth. And working with developed – or more developed – countries can provide poorer countries with much-needed expertise and access to advanced technologies. The downside is that there are limits, or diminishing returns: a developing country simply may not have the capacity to use lots of aid – for example, the government may not be large enough to manage multiple projects or there may not be enough teachers to staff newly built schools.

No, aid doesn't promote growth (and can even undermine it): In this, the most negative, scenario, aid is seen as a source of corruption and a way of enriching the elites in developing countries. It is, in the words of one critic, "an excellent method for transferring money from poor people in rich countries to rich people in poor countries". Aid critics also argue, with some justification, that aid cuts the line of accountability between governments and citizens: "Rather than forge a productive relationship with their own citizens, governments find it more profitable to negotiate for revenues from abroad," argues Andrew Mwenda, a Ugandan journalist and aid critic. He goes further, and argues that "by providing them an external subsidy, governments in Africa have been able to retain power even when pursuing policies that impoverish their citizens." Such criticisms have been heard more widely in recent years, sparking a debate on how best to ensure that aid doesn't undermine government accountability. As we'll see in Chapter 7, they've also helped promote ideas for strengthening the relationship between governments and citizens, through, for example, the development of national tax systems.

Aid, it's also argued, risks causing "Dutch disease", where an influx of capital causes the value of a developing country's currency to rise, so making its exports more expensive and harming competitiveness *(see Chapter 2)*. But, because aid flows are usually fairly small in relation to overall economic activity, the effect is probably pretty minimal. And any loss in the manufacturing sector is likely to be made up by increased productivity as a result of rising levels of education and health. However, such improvements are likely to happen only over the longer term; by contrast, aid flows to individual countries can rise and fall quite sharply. Where that happens, Dutch disease may well be a risk and may not be offset by the longer-term benefits. That's one reason why aid needs to be predictable, allowing developing countries to plan based on long-term donor commitments.

> "Effective tax systems, based on co-operative relationships between governments, businesses and individuals, are a bedrock for democracy and growth."
> Angel Gurría, OECD Secretary-General

Yes, aid promotes growth (but only in the right circumstances): This, more nuanced, scenario, looks at aid within its real-world contexts, which can limit – or bolster – its effectiveness. These contexts relate to three main areas:

> The nature of the recipient country – for example, how well it's governed; its policies in trade and other areas; its existing level of development; its tendency towards conflict; its track record on human rights and free speech, and so on.

> How donors "do" aid – do they work through the recipient government and co-ordinate with other donors, or take a go-it-alone approach? Do they stick to aid commitments? Do they monitor and evaluate aid effectively?

> The type of aid – emergency relief, for example, is unlikely to drive economic growth; rather, its arrival often coincides with events, like earthquakes or floods, that can knock an economy to the floor. Aid aimed at improving health and education or the quality of governance probably promotes growth, but its effects are so long term that they can be hard to demonstrate. By contrast, a more immediate result is likely to be seen with aid aimed at strengthening infrastructure – building bridges and roads or supplying electricity.

To sum up, all of these scenarios – "yes", "no", and "yes, but" – have been supported by various studies. But in recent years, there's been

5. Are we getting results?

a growing consensus around the third scenario – aid does indeed promote economic growth, *but* it needs the right circumstances. There's much speculation on why studies now tend to show a link between aid and growth: it may be that researchers now use more effective methods and have greater access to a growing body of data. Or it may be that recipient and donor governments are now thinking more about how to get the most out of aid. Indeed, and as we'll see in the next chapter, there's been a substantial focus in recent years on making aid more effective through strengthening the quality of institutions and governance in recipient countries and rethinking donors' aid practices.

The impact on the ground

Unlike the question of its economic impact, the case for the impact of development co-operation on the ground is easier to make. There is no shortage of examples: if you've ever donated money to an NGO working in a developing country, you've probably received a newsletter explaining how your donation helped to dig a well or build a school. On a larger scale, there are some outstanding examples of how development initiatives have improved people's lives.

One of the most famous is the eradication of smallpox. In the 18th century, smallpox claimed the lives of one in ten children in France and one in seven in Russia. But the invention of vaccination by Edward Jenner at the end of the 18th century, helped put the disease on the run in Europe and North America. In many poor countries, however, it remained a killer, claiming 1.5 million lives a year even into the mid-1950s. That was when the WHO began a global push to wipe out the disease, backed by an eventual $98 million in funding. In 1977 in Somalia, smallpox claimed its last natural victim (a laboratory accident led to one more death in 1978), and became the only infectious human disease to date to have been fully eradicated. Other diseases have yet to be vanquished, but their impact has been greatly diminished: River blindness was a devastating disease in much of West Africa up to the mid-1970s, blinding up to one in twenty adults in the worst affected areas, typically communities living in river valleys. But, beginning in 1974, a programme that would eventually be backed by funding worth more than $500 million began making huge progress against the disease. By early in the new millennium, its transmission had been halted in 11 West African countries, and an estimated half a million cases had been prevented.

There are countless other examples of aid successes – both official and private. In health, China, backed by The World Bank and the WHO, launched a campaign against tuberculosis in the early 1990s in its worst-affected provinces. Nineteen out of twenty new cases of TB were successfully treated using the innovative DOTS (Directly Observed Treatment Short Course) programme, which closely monitors patients during treatment to ensure they take their drugs, at a cost of less than $100 per person. In nutrition, much of the work that laid the foundations for the Green Revolution – which saw Mexico, Pakistan and India go from net food importers to net exporters in the space of a decade – was funded by the Rockefeller and Ford foundations, US-based philanthropic groups. In education, "considerable" donor financing in Sub-Saharan Africa has led to an "explosion" in school enrolment in the region over the past few years, according to a UNESCO report.

But if aid has done some good at the micro level, critics argue it has also at times done harm. They point to donor funding of controversial projects like the construction of hydroelectric dams, which may displace villagers and endanger the ecosystems of lakes and rivers. In recent years, there's also been a debate over the impact of humanitarian aid in war-torn regions, with claims that it may in some cases be "subsidising" and extending conflicts. Journalist Philip Gourevitch sums up the case: "Humanitarianism relieves the warring parties of many of the burdens (administrative and financial) of waging war, diminishing the demands of governing while fighting, cutting the cost of sustaining casualties, and supplying the food, medicine, and logistical support that keep armies going."

And even though aid can bring short-term benefits, these sometimes need to be weighed against longer-term losses, especially the development of sustainable, local solutions in developing countries. Where local healthcare is not up to the mark, it may seem to make sense to "ship in trained doctors from abroad and set up projects separate from local and quite possibly inefficient health systems to get lots of people immunized fast, to get the job done," as Jonathan Glennie has noted. But, as he also points out, such approaches can "undermine the building of a sustainable health system to serve the population in the years ahead … [and] erode public trust in national systems, which takes years to build". It may also lead local staff, quite reasonably, to desert local jobs and instead seek out higher-paying work in donor agencies, further weakening the national system.

What does the public think?

In policy terms, the position of development aid is probably unique. In any other policy area, a government can promise voters that they will enjoy direct benefits from its actions – for instance, spending on the environment can be justified in terms of fresher air or cleaner water; spending on education can be "sold" as a way of improving individuals' economic prospects, and so on. But this is not really the case with development aid. It's true that people in developed countries can one day expect to see benefits from rising prosperity in developing countries, for example through the creation of new markets and enhanced security. But those benefits are indirect and not immediate; instead, the direct and immediate beneficiaries of development aid are people living in other countries and not the citizens and taxpayers of governments making the policy decision.

In political science, there's a name for this issue: the **principal-agent problem**. In this instance, you as a taxpayer and citizen are the principal and your country's government is your agent. When you pay your taxes, you expect something in return – water piped to your home, for example. If the water stops running, you can complain to the government or vote for someone else at the next election. So, between the principal (you) and the agent (the government) there's a feedback loop – you can tell the government what you think of its water services, and the government can offer its apologies and try to make things better, or suffer the electoral consequences.

In aid, this loop doesn't really exist. Citizens in donor countries pay taxes in the expectation that their agent, the government, will distribute some of it wisely through assistance. But if that money is not used well, if it fails to achieve development goals, the would-be beneficiaries have no real way of letting you know. This problem doesn't just exist in the relationship between taxpayers and their government. It's there at every stage of the aid chain – for example, when a government acting as a principal provides funding to an aid agency (the agent) or between a donor and a recipient government.

This might sound like a minor issue, but it has many real-world implications. One is that governments and NGOs must "sell" the idea of aid to people in developed countries, and monitor their mood. Some people argue that this can lead to a narrow focus in demonstrating aid effectiveness – one that steers aid towards showing results for the sake of showing results, rather than supporting longer-term, more sustainable development processes.

Public opinion and aid

Public opinion on aid can be contradictory: on the one hand, voters generally support aid; on the other, they often overestimate its scale. The headline from one blog posting sums up some of these contradictions: "Americans appalled at how much we spend on aid, want to spend 10 times more." That's reference to a poll in the United States in 2010 in which respondents estimated that about a quarter of the entire Federal budget went on foreign aid. Asked if they thought that was too much, most said yes, and said the budget share should be about 10%. But even that is still about ten times more than the actual figure of less than 1%. There's similar confusion in Europe: in a 2007 survey, only about 6% of respondents in the new EU states came close to guessing how much the European and EU Member Countries give in aid. The public also often shows signs of scepticism towards what aid can achieve, and is especially worried about the impact of corruption in recipient countries: in a survey in France, 53% of respondents cited it as the first or second most important barrier to aid effectiveness, while in the United Kingdom, 52% of respondents said "corruption in poor country governments makes it pointless donating money to help reduce poverty".

Despite such confusion and doubts, public opinion towards aid is generally fairly upbeat in OECD countries, and has remained so despite the economic turmoil of the past few years. Survey after survey shows strong support for the idea of development co-operation: in a 2009 EU survey, for instance, 72% of respondents backed honouring or exceeding existing aid commitments to developing countries. Yet, as the report also noted, "Europeans have little understanding of the workings of development co-operation, [although] they have a genuine interest in knowing more".

5. Are we getting results?

The need to win public support in OECD countries for development co-operation has long been recognised, as has the need to educate the public. These needs will only grow if governments decide to raise aid levels to speed progress towards the Millennium Development Goals (MDGs). And yet public knowledge is weak – most people in surveys, for instance, say they believe most aid goes on humanitarian relief and emergencies; in fact, as we've seen, such aid accounts for only a small proportion of overall ODA. Communicating the achievements of aid has also been complicated by the evolving nature of the aid world in recent years: The "professionalisation" of aid and emergence of an aid "industry" – for want of a better word – means discussion is often "cloaked in jargon and technicality", as one OECD report put it. The focus of aid has also evolved, with donors increasingly channelling aid through recipient governments, which can make it difficult to attribute success to individual donors. This may enable the recipient to use aid more effectively, but makes it harder for donor governments to show results that will convince their citizens to support further spending.

> "Maintaining and strengthening public support for aid can be facilitated by more effective communication of its role in the development process and the successes that, in combination with recipients' own self-help efforts, aid has achieved …"
>
> *Development Co-operation Report 1985*

Some donors are increasingly trying to communicate with their publics in ways that link their aid activities to general improvements in developing countries – in effect, they're trying to communicate "the big picture", rather than focusing on smaller successes. But there's still a danger that in order to have some story to tell, governments and especially NGOs may pursue short-term "wins" rather than longer-term, but harder to measure, achievements. Indeed, there's concern in some circles that the measures of development success increasingly favour such quick victories. Critics argue that obsessively setting targets and metrics for development co-operation can mean that resources are steered towards programmes with easily measurable results rather than those where success may be harder to determine, but which have perhaps a potential to bring about longer-term progress. "How does an aid manager measure the impact of the new constitution written with technical assistance," writes Andrew Natsios, a former US aid official, "or an anti-corruption program, or support for an indigenous think tank or research centre?"

Critics also argue that because of the broken feedback loop in aid, there's insufficient incentive for officials in aid agencies to worry about the impact of programmes and projects: even if they're successful, that message won't make it back home. Workers at Sweden's aid agency, for example, estimated that only 2% of promotions reflected the success of projects that staff had worked on in the past, according to a study in the early 2000s. By contrast, research tends to suggest that aid staff may focus on tasks that can easily be monitored, such as hiring and procurement, rather than delivering actual benefits. These issues underline why evaluation is important – there does need to be some measurement of whether aid programmes and projects are actually working. In the final section of this chapter, we'll look at some of the ways in which that's done.

How is success or failure measured?

The idea of systematically evaluating aid is not new – the OECD's principles for aid evaluation (see next section) date back to 1991, for example. But it has received a fresh impetus in recent years in the wake of the financial crisis, which has put severe pressure on government spending in many traditional donor countries. Many governments feel that now, more than ever, aid needs to demonstrate that it's delivering value for money.

> **"Pressure on aid budgets and new approaches to development assistance have increased the demands on evaluation as a key component of the accountability, management and learning structures of development agencies."**
>
> Jon Lomøy, Evaluation in Development Agencies, December 2010

But even though the idea of aid evaluation has been around for some time, it's still something of a work in progress – there is extensive debate over how it should be done, and what its main focus should be: should it concentrate mainly on accountability, in other words, saying where resources went and what happened to them? Or should it aim to try to produce lessons for future work? Of course, neither of these ideas – or any of the other approaches in aid evaluation – are mutually exclusive. Nevertheless, it's worth bearing in mind that there are a number of different theories and philosophies in aid evaluation.

Criteria used for evaluation

This said, some ideas have been very widely adopted. In particular, there's a lot of agreement on the criteria for evaluation: in other words, what an aid project or programme should be able to show in order to be judged a success. Although the terminology can vary, the criteria for aid evaluation are generally based around the following ideas formulated by the OECD Development Assistance Committee (DAC):

Relevance: Is the aid activity suited to the priorities and needs of the people it's supposed to be helping and to the capacities of the donor? Relevance also asks if the objectives of a programme remain valid – they may have been once, but are they still? And it asks how well the actual output of a programme matches up with the intended impact.

Effectiveness: Simply, to what extent have the objectives been met? If they haven't been fully met, why not?

Efficiency: In simple terms, how big a bang are you getting for your buck? Or, how much was spent in terms of time and resources compared to how much was achieved? In most projects – in development and more widely – there's any number of ways to achieve the same result, some using relatively few resources and some much more. The test of an efficient result is if it was achieved using the approach that involved the least resources. If that approach wasn't taken, why not?

Impact: What has changed, both good and bad, as a result of a development intervention, and why? Judging the scale of a programme's impact can be difficult. For example, typically, an aid project is thought to affect only people living in the target area. But that's not necessarily always the case: if a village benefits from a new well or a clinic, the local government may decide to shift resources to another village, in which case the project can have a wider, indirect effect.

Sustainability: Will the benefits of an intervention continue even after donor funding ends? Also, is it environmentally sustainable? Unless proper systems are in place, the impacts of aid projects can be quite limited: for example, a scheme to raise child nutrition works only for as long as children are receiving a proper diet. For the benefits to continue, it must gain a sustainable foothold, with support that can be maintained even after donor funding ends.

Principles for aid evaluation

Twenty years ago, the OECD produced a set of principles aimed at improving aid evaluation, and these have become influential in shaping the way aid projects and programmes are thought about. To those not directly involved in development work, some of these principles can seem rather technical. But others are easily understood, and can help give a sense of how aid evaluation can be made to work.

For example, one of the OECD principles calls for evaluations to be **credible**, reporting failure as well as success. The fact that aid sometimes fails is hardly surprising. (Overall, data from donors suggests that between about a tenth and a quarter of projects "fail," in the sense of not fully meeting objectives.) After all, even in developed countries, government projects don't always meet expectations, despite excellent infrastructure and access to huge amounts of information and data. In business, too, failure is hardly rare: in the United States, research suggests that only about 44% of new businesses survive their first four years. In developing countries, conditions can be far more difficult, and the odds may be stacked against success. Identifying failure is important from the perspective of accountability, but also from the perspective of learning, both for ongoing and future projects.

Although there has sometimes been a perception that aid's failures were swept under the carpet, this view is becoming less valid. Among NGOs, for instance, a group called Engineers Without Borders has set up the self-explanatory website *admittingfailures.com* with the specific aim of providing a forum for people in development to learn from each other's mistakes. And official evaluations also can be quite frank about failures: One investigation into conflict prevention and peace-building activities in Southern Sudan describes donors' efforts as only "partially successful" and criticises them for relying on approaches that – according to development theory – should be effective, but which in reality and in this case didn't work. "Donors have placed too much emphasis on standard Western 'good practice' models promoted by foreign experts unfamiliar with Southern Sudan," it states. Recognising such failures can be an uncomfortable experience, but it's essential if lessons are to be learnt and if evaluation is to be credible. Providing such recognition is easier when evaluations are carried out **impartially** – another of the OECD principles – either by independent units in aid agencies or by outside consultants. When evaluating impact, it is also important to look at why something did or did not work, to be able to extend a successful initiative or not repeat mistakes in future.

> "Independence helps ensure the credibility and objectiveness of evaluation…"
>
> *Evaluation in Development Agencies, December 2010*

The principles emphasise a number of other important ideas: these include **inclusiveness** – in other words, a donor country or agency shouldn't just evaluate an aid action from its own perspective, but should also involve representatives of the recipient side of the equation. Another is **dissemination**, or ensuring that findings are as widely distributed as possible in order to generate feedback and to maximise the opportunities for learning lessons.

Working towards a deeper partnership

This chapter has dipped a toe into the huge question of whether or not aid works, and has looked at some of the ways in which this question is investigated systematically by aid agencies and governments. The growing body of research on these issues has had a major impact on how recipients and donors "do" aid, and, as we'll see in the next chapter, has led to substantial efforts to deepen the development co-operation partnership.

Find Out More

FROM OECD ...

On the Internet

To find out about OECD work on **aid evaluation** and for links to the **DAC Network on Development Evaluation**, go to *www.oecd.org/dac/evaluation*.

A wide range of development evaluation reports from donor agencies can be found at the DEReC website at *www.oecd.org/dac/evaluationnetwork/derec*.

For an introduction to **communications, public opinion and development**, go to *www.oecd.org/dev/devcom*. Learn about **DevCom**, an informal network bringing together the public affairs and communication directors of a number of development ministries and official agencies at *www.oecd.org/dataoecd/6/7/46271455.pdf*.

Publications

Quality Standards for Development Evaluation (2010): Provides a guide to good practice in development evaluation, with the aim of improving the quality of evaluation processes and products and facilitating collaboration.

Evaluating Development Co-operation (2010): A summary of international norms and standards for development evaluation.

Evaluation in Development Agencies (2010; in the "Better Aid" series): The evaluation of official development programmes has grown tremendously over the past two decades amid increasing public demand for credible assessments of whether aid "works" to improve the lives of the world's poorest. Drawing from a range of sources, including questionnaires and peer reviews by the OECD DAC, this study describes the role and management of evaluation in development agencies and multilateral banks.

Glossary of Key Terms in Evaluation and Results-Based Management (2010): This useful glossary clarifies concepts and aims to reduce the confusion over terminology that's frequently encountered in these areas. Covers the following languages: English, French, Spanish, Arabic, Chinese, Dutch, German, Italian, Japanese, Portuguese, Kiswahili, Korean, Russian, Swedish, Turkish.

... AND OTHER SOURCES

Living Proof (*www.one.org/livingproof*): Supported by the Gates Foundation, Living Proof showcases stories of success in development.

Blogs

The "does aid work?" debate is well represented on the blogosphere. In the pro-aid camp, one of the leading figures is **Jeffrey Sachs** of Colombia University. The author of the highly influential *The End of Poverty* (2005) is also chair of The Earth Institute and a special advisor to UN Secretary-General Ban Ki-moon. Prof. Sachs blogs regularly at *www.huffingtonpost.com/jeffrey-sachs*. There's a range of views on aid and development issues on display at *The Guardian's* **Poverty Matters Blog** (*www.guardian.co.uk/global-development/poverty-matters*), with regular contributions from Jonathan Glennie, author of *The Trouble With Aid* (2008). Sadly, one of the most widely read blogs with a sceptical leaning has pulled down its shutters. But the **Aidwatch blog** (at *http://aidwatchers.com*) – which is most associated with William Easterly, author of *The White Man's Burden* (2006) – is worth looking at for its archive of lively postings and useful links to other development blogs.

6

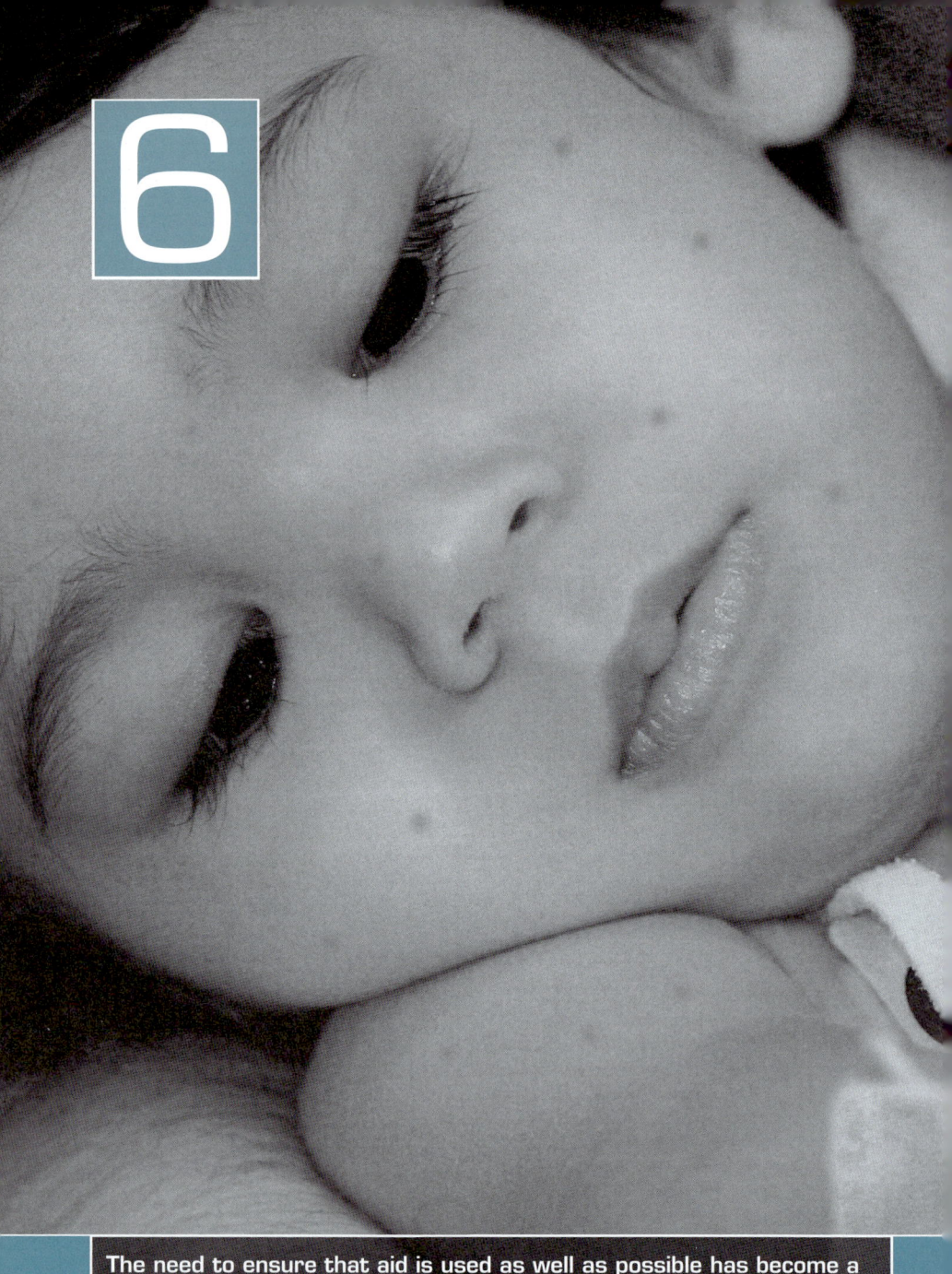

The need to ensure that aid is used as well as possible has become a dominant theme in development. Making this happen requires a new relationship between developing and developed countries. Partnership is key, not just in aid but in a range of policy areas.

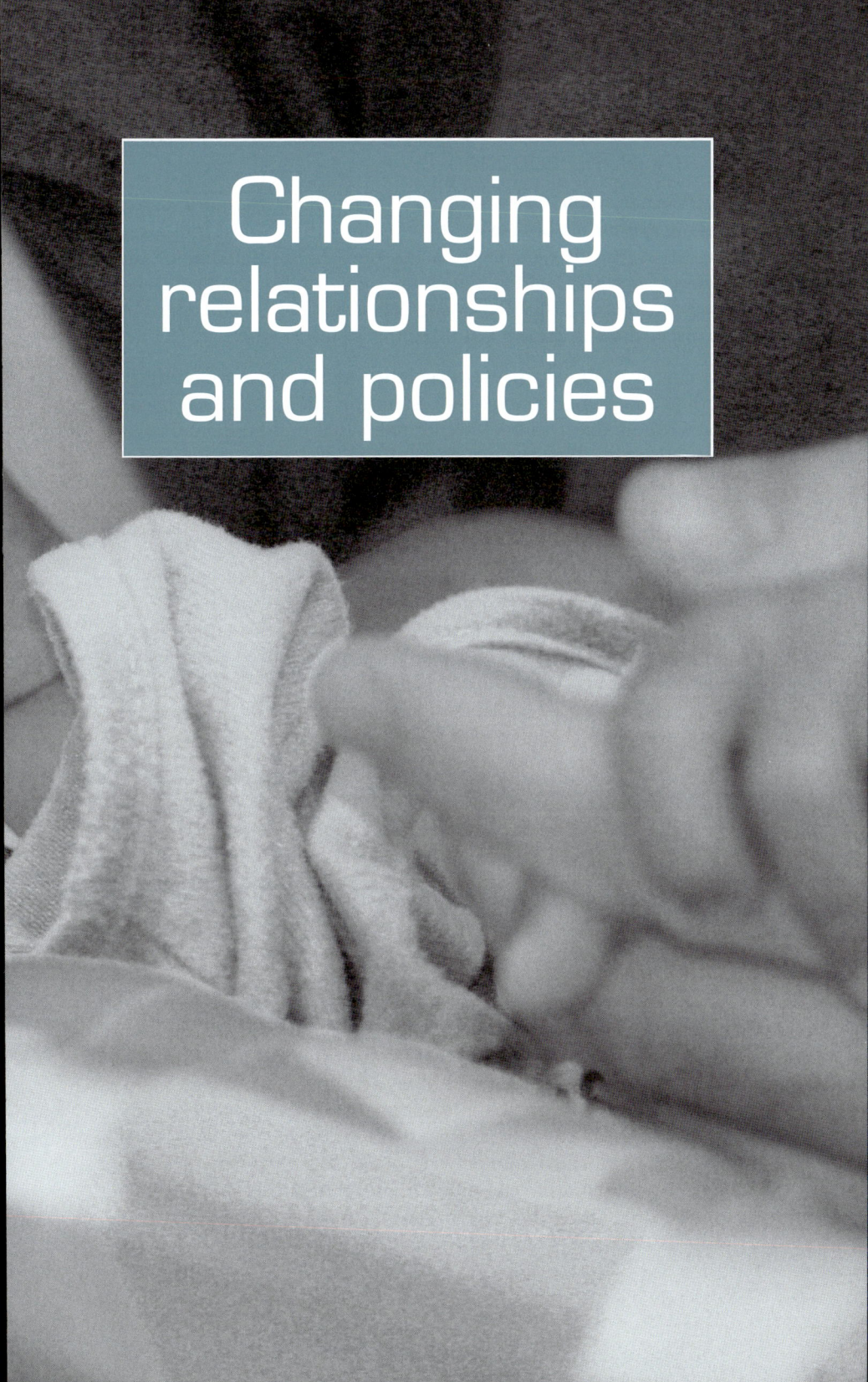

Changing relationships and policies

By way of introduction …

In February 2005, a young girl in northern Sumatra began showing symptoms of measles. At the time, this part of Indonesia was still trying to recover from the devastating tsunami of the previous December, which had claimed tens of thousands of lives, wiped out towns and villages and left many people homeless. A measles outbreak was the last thing the region needed.

Fearing an outbreak, disease specialists raced to examine the girl. But then something strange happened: the girl's symptoms began to fade. Soon, she was back to normal. What had happened? The explanation was this: the girl had suffered a reaction to a measles vaccination. But it hadn't been given just once. Amid the chaos of the post-tsunami clear up, the girl had been vaccinated three times, by three different organisations. Little wonder she fell ill.

The story of the measles case that never was has attained a certain notoriety in development circles. It represents the reality that, despite the best intentions, the delivery of aid is not always as effective as it might be. Scarce resources may be wasted, sometimes through genuine mix-ups, as happened in Indonesia, and sometimes as a result of bribery and corruption. Indeed, as the aid world has become ever more complex, the scope for such problems has only grown.

In response, there's been a concerted effort in the international community to ensure that aid is used as effectively as possible. This effort is based in large part on the core idea that developing countries should take charge of their own development agendas, co-ordinating the work of multiple donors and providing the systems and mechanisms for ensuring that aid reaches those who need it most.

This represents a major shift in the relationship between developing countries and donors, one that positions them increasingly as partners. But that partnership goes beyond aid. As we've seen, developing and donor countries interact in many different ways – through trade, financial flows, investment and much more. All these can shape the prospects of developing countries. If the development co-operation partnership is to be really meaningful, the development impact of policies needs to be taken into account.

6. Changing relationships and policies

▶ This chapter looks at how we can get the most out of development co-operation. How can aid be made more effective? How can we treat the cancer of corruption, which eats not only into the effectiveness of aid and public spending in developing countries, but also into the confidence of voters in donor countries? And how can we ensure that the partnership between donors and developing countries works through a full range of policy areas – trade, investment, and so on – and not just through the narrow focus of aid?

How can aid be made more effective?

Over the past decade or so, aid effectiveness – or making aid work better – has "become a central notion in the lexicon of the aid industry," as Daniel Kaufmann of the Brookings Institute puts it. Unfortunately, jargon and specialist terminology has meant that much of the discussion in this area can be inaccessible to people outside "the aid industry". That's a pity: aid effectiveness matters because it really can make a concrete contribution to development.

On a basic level, aid effectiveness might seem to be about getting maximum bang for the donor's buck. That's one goal, but it isn't the only one. The much broader agenda has been to recast the relationship between donor and recipient countries as a partnership. That has important implications: in a partnership, each side needs to be accountable to the other; each side also needs to avoid undercutting the other's efforts.

The Paris Declaration on Aid Effectiveness

Many of these ideas can be examined through the lens of the Paris Declaration, which was adopted in 2005 at a conference of donor and developing countries. The Paris Declaration has been described as essentially technocratic. Unlike the Millennium Development Goals (MDGs), for instance, it doesn't set targets for development, like halving extreme poverty (*see Chapter 2*). Instead, it sets goals for "doing" development co-operation; in other words, how should donors and developing countries work together to meet their goals and maximise the impact of aid. That, in itself, is a complicated idea, and may not have much resonance for people outside the aid world. Nevertheless, the declaration's five principles – ownership, alignment, harmonisation, results and mutual accountability – do provide an entry point for discussing some of the main challenges in making aid more effective.

Ownership: The core idea behind ownership is this: it should be up to each developing country to set its own development goals, map out the route to reaching them, and co-ordinate its own and donors' activities. In some ways, it's surprising that this idea even needs to be explained: it's hard to imagine a developed country like France or Australia allowing its health or education policy to be dictated by another country. The same is true for developing countries, as the scholar Roger Riddell points out: "In a nutshell, if governments do not own these programmes and are not committed to them, then – it is now almost universally agreed – they are almost bound to fail."

> "Aid is more effective when partner countries exercise strong and effective leadership over their development policies and strategies."
> *Development Co-operation Report 2005*

In many ways, ownership is the key idea in aid effectiveness – without it, none of the other principles can really work. Ownership aims to make the government of each developing country accountable primarily to its own people and parliament, not to its donors. This may not happen overnight: in some developing countries, systems of democratic accountability – regardless of how they're defined – are still relatively weak. Parliaments may not be able to exercise adequate oversight and civil society may be relatively underdeveloped and, in some cases, suppressed. But even the act of holding governments – and not donors – accountable can play a role in developing these processes. On the donor side, ownership implies an expectation of relying more on things like the civil service, budgetary processes and data collection of the recipient country, rather than setting up parallel systems. When it works well, ownership should create a virtuous circle that strengthens a developing country's ability to manage its own affairs. That, in itself, is development.

Alongside some of the other principles of aid effectiveness, ownership also offers the hope of reducing the chaotic aspect of aid.

As we've seen, aid is characterised by a vast, and growing, number of agencies and operators, and their activities don't always blend well with each other or with what the developing country is trying to do. Increasingly, the solution is seen as encouraging developing countries to take the lead in co-ordinating such activities.

And yet, despite widespread acceptance of the principle, ownership is still enmeshed in some contentious issues. One is that donor and developing governments have not always agreed on what ownership actually means. When the idea first began to emerge in the 1980s, donors tended to regard "ownership" as the process of developing countries taking on board their – the donors' – policy advice. By contrast, developing countries tended to see it more as the extent to which they had control of the agenda.

Such debates are heard less often these days, but that's not to say that the meaning of ownership is entirely settled. For example there's continuing discussion over *who* should exercise ownership in developing countries – government or the people who will be directly affected by aid initiatives? Over the past decade or so, representatives of communities or social groups – or civil society – have indeed gained a stronger voice in the debate, and have become increasingly visible at international conferences on aid effectiveness. However, research suggests they have had only mixed success in gaining a policy role in a number of developing countries.

When it comes to developing countries "claiming" ownership, some may find it easier than others. This can reflect perceptions – and realities – of weak governance, with donors less willing to yield control to countries with relatively poor track records. But it can also reflect other factors, including the relative "balance of power" between donor and recipient governments. For example, Viet Nam has emerged as a "donor darling" in recent years: it has a strong government, booming economy and a proven track record of development achievement. Donors are attracted to Viet Nam – it's one of the world's largest recipients of Overseas Development Aid (ODA) in cash terms – and this has helped to strengthen the country's hand in setting its own aid agenda. Viet Nam has created its own version of the Paris Declaration, the Hanoi Core Statement, and it has not been afraid to reject aid if it comes with what the government sees as unacceptable conditions.

By contrast, some other countries, especially in Sub-Saharan Africa, find it harder to assert ownership. Arguably this may reflect a long history of somewhat one-sided engagement between countries and donors. As a former president of Mozambique, Joaquim Chissano, has noted: "For each African country in general, the lead donor was the former colonial power, who commanded a lot of influence over other donors and their attitude towards the former colony." More recently, in the 1970s and 1980s, many developing countries became very reliant on support from the International Monetary Fund (IMF) and The World Bank, which in turn took on a substantial role in shaping policy. Those habits have not always been easy to overturn.

" … While volumes of aid and other development resources are increasing to achieve [Vietnam's Development Goals], aid effectiveness must also increase significantly to support Vietnam's efforts to strengthen governance, to improve development performance, and to enhance development outcomes."

Hanoi Core Statement, 2011

It's also important to recognise that establishing ownership can be difficult if donors and recipients don't see the world in the same way. As Joaquim Chissano has stated, "In some cases, the priorities of donors and recipients do not match; an example of this is the construction of infrastructure in Africa, viewed by the Africans as a high priority for their sustainable development and systematically dismissed by donors." Indeed, such differences of approach are often cited as one reason why African governments increasingly turn to donors like China, who can be receptive to funding and building things like new roads and bridges, while "traditional" donors have been more focused in recent years on issues such as health and education.

Alignment: The terminology of aid effectiveness can be a little opaque, and the distinctions between some of the most widely used terms may not always be immediately apparent. This isn't simply a question of language; it also reflects the interlocking nature of the core principles – for each of them to work fully requires that the others, too, come into play. Take the examples of ownership and alignment. As we've seen, ownership is essentially about a developing country taking control of its own development agenda and setting down its own plans. But that can only happen fully if its donors respond by *aligning* their activities with those plans. Hence the principle of alignment. This goes beyond simply following the developing country's plans; it also asks donors to use the developing country's own financial and budgetary systems in order that the people and their representatives in parliament, as well as civil society and the media, can get a clear picture of what is being planned and how money is being spent.

> " ... when donors pursue their own projects and programmes and bypass the administrative systems, policies and priorities of the partner country in which they are involved, the sustainability of their efforts is undermined, as well as the ability of the countries receiving aid to manage their own future."
> Brenda Killen, *OECD Journal: General Papers*

One of the most discussed issues in alignment is **aid predictability** – in other words, does the developing country know how much it will receive in aid over the next one to three years? Why does this matter? Aid successes are sometimes represented as one-offs – the building of a school or a hospital. But, in practice, most of the cost of a school or a hospital is recurring: it's not enough just to build four walls and a roof; you also need to hire teachers or medical staff and then pay them year in and year out. Unless support from donors is predictable, it's hard to commit sustainably to such spending. Unfortunately, aid is often not predictable. According to analysis of IMF-supported programmes between 1990 and 2005, about 30% of aid destined to support developing countries' budgets did not meet predictions.

Harmonisation: Managing relations with a donor requires an investment of time and resources by developing countries. And, because most of them have more than one donor, this task is usually multiplied many times. In Tanzania in the early part of the last decade, officials were reported to be writing 2 000 reports for donors every year and receiving 1 000 donor missions. Things got so bad that the government had to declare a four-month "mission holiday" to let ministers and officials get on with their regular jobs.

Such incidents are by no means isolated. Aid, as one OECD Development Centre report notes, was once "a tiny club affair, reserved to a small number of partnerships". But, as we've seen repeatedly in this book, the arrival of new donors and the influx of non-governmental organisations (NGOs) in recent decades mean that's no longer the case. In 2007, it's estimated that there were at least 90 000 aid projects running worldwide, many of which would have required some level of reporting by the bureaucracies of developing countries.

The proliferation of donors can lead to other problems: the aid economist Paul Collier recalls a case in Africa where three donor agencies decided to build a hospital in the same place. "They agreed to co-ordinate, which doesn't always happen," he writes, "but then faced the problem of having three incompatible sets of rules for how the work should be commissioned. It took them two years to reach a compromise, which was that each agency should build one floor of the hospital under its own rules. You can imagine how efficient that was likely to be."

In many countries, it also isn't clear what exactly donors – and NGOs – are doing. In Malawi, a health official was trying to make a decision on where to locate new clinics: "With tiny budgets, the health department strives for maximum impact by building new clinics close to under-served populations," writes Owen Barder of the Centre for Global Development. They know the location of state facilities, "but can't find out where donors and NGOs have put their clinics and where they plan to build new ones."

> "Managing for results means managing and implementing aid in a way that focuses on the desired results and uses information to improve decision making."
>
> Paris Declaration on Aid Effectiveness

The idea behind harmonisation in aid effectiveness is to tackle these problems by getting donors to work together better. One approach has been to reduce **aid fragmentation**, which is basically just another way of cutting the number of donors operating in each country. This can be done in several different ways: Donors can focus their efforts on just a few countries; channel aid through agencies like the UN; or allow one donor to take the lead role with financial support from others. Greater **transparency** is also important to harmonisation, firstly to allow greater co-ordination of aid efforts but, secondly, as Owen Barder notes, because "citizens of developing countries are entitled to know how aid is spent in their country."

Results: Aid can also be made more effective if both donors and recipients think in terms of what they are trying to achieve, or, in the jargon of the aid business, if they are "managing for development results". In recent years, many governments have zeroed in on the idea of "results-based management" to promote good governance – in other words: "Clear objectives, evidence-based decision making, transparency and continuous improvement," as one OECD report puts it. Development is no exception, and it's increasingly subject to the sort of management approaches pioneered in the private sector – extensive planning, constant monitoring and evaluation, and systemised approaches to learning lessons from both failures and successes.

Mutual accountability: The aid relationship has often been represented as a form of the "principal-agent" accountability model *(see previous chapter)*, with donors as the principals and developing countries as the agent. Frequently, this involved donors providing aid in return for the recipient accepting certain conditions aimed at improving – at least in the donor's eyes – the politics and behaviour of the developing country. Conditionality hasn't gone away, but increasingly this sort of one-sided relationship is regarded as outmoded and unhelpful. For one thing, it makes the developing country's government accountable to donors, not to its own citizens. For another, conditionality is widely seen as having done little to change how developing countries do things.

> "The overriding impression is that conditionality has largely been ineffective in enhancing the impact of development aid on growth or human development."
> Andrew Mold, *Policy Ownership and Aid Conditionality in the Light of the Financial Crisis* (2009)

The idea of mutual accountability is to make donors and recipients accountable to each other through individual and joint actions. Developing countries, for example, are expected to work to strengthen oversight by their own parliaments; donors are expected to provide transparent information on aid flows so that governments in developing countries can provide comprehensive budget information to their own parliament and people; and the two sides together are expected to jointly assess their success, or otherwise, in meeting development goals.

The way we used to do it is not the way we do it now

Talking about ideas like ownership – and the other principles of aid effectiveness – is easy, but it only begins to matter if the talk is translated into reality. So, are donors and recipients really changing the way they "do" development co-operation? "I've been in aid management since 2001, and the way we used to do it is not the way we do it now," Twaib Ali, a senior official in Malawi's finance ministry, told the OECD. "Then, we looked at our development partners as donors, but the Paris Declaration has changed that perception." Indeed, that view seems to be widely shared, among both developing and developed countries: "Compared with the aid situation 20 to 25 years ago current practice presents a global picture of far greater transparency and far less donor-driven aid today," states a major Danish-led evaluation of the Paris Declaration. "The 'free-for-alls' of competitive, uncoordinated and donor-driven activities that were commonplace at that time are now unusual enough to attract rapid attention and criticism."

> "The reasons why donors have often insisted on such a dominant role are not hard to understand. Some of the least-developed countries have lacked the political or administrative institutions to support aid projects, or have suffered from such high levels of corruption that donor countries have not felt confident about channelling funding through official channels."
>
> *Development Co-operation Report 2009*

But the change has not gone far enough, says Twaib Ali: "Unfortunately, some of the development partners are not forthcoming on delivering on some of the agreed principles. For instance, very few are willing to use our country systems. … That is weakening us, because then we are not owning those programmes. We know our country systems are not that perfect, but the moment they start using our country systems [they will strengthen]." Indeed, it's fair to say that the developing countries are seen as having gone further in changing the way they do things than the donors. That's clear even in some of the processes that surround the Paris Declaration. Since it was adopted, its successes and failures have been monitored in special surveys, each of which has attracted a growing number of developing country participants – from just 34 in the first survey to 91 in the most recent.

Many donors have been less enthusiastic, although there are exceptions. Irish Aid, the official agency in Ireland, is praised in one evaluation for its "high" commitment to the aid effectiveness principles: "Staff understand and own not just the letter but the spirit of these principles." But other donors have made rather less progress. Why? There are many reasons, not the least of which is that donors may be risk averse, and unwilling to change the way they do things. Donors may also question whether a developing country has the capacity – both political and administrative – to handle aid initiatives. And there may be concerns about allowing corrupt governments in some developing countries to exert high levels of control over donor funds. "Corrupt practices continue to frustrate the best intentions and objectives of more effective aid and limit the potential for better partnerships," states the Danish evaluation. Indeed, as we've seen, such concerns are shared by voters in donor countries. Are these fears justified? We'll explore that question next.

What is the impact of corruption on development?

Corruption happens everywhere, in rich countries and in poor. That's not to say the problem is on the same scale everywhere – it's not. As surveys like Transparency International's Corruption Perceptions Index show, poorer countries tend to have worse track records for graft. "Corruption is pervasive and persistent in Africa," Léonce Ndikumana of the African Development Bank has stated. "The cost of corruption to economic activity and growth is staggering." But even among developed countries, some are "cleaner" than others. So, corruption is not just a developing country problem. Equally, it's not just an aid problem. In the words of the Partnership Declaration adopted by developed and developing countries at the High-Level Forum on Aid Effectiveness in Busan, Korea, in late 2011: "Corruption is a plague that seriously undermines development globally, diverting resources that could be harnessed to finance development, damaging the quality of governance institutions, and threatening human security." In many countries, corruption is endemic and aid gets caught up with it, like any other financial transaction. That said, and as we'll see a little later, a case can be made for saying that in certain circumstances aid can feed corruption.

As we saw in the previous chapter, surveys in donor countries indicate that the public believes corruption is a major – perhaps *the* major – obstacle to aid effectiveness. Corruption's secretive nature, which makes it impossible to accurately gauge, means it's hard to say if those concerns are fully justified. But even if they're not, there's no doubt that corruption does mean that some aid funds don't wind up where they're supposed to go. There's also no doubt that the growing efforts in recent years to tackle such problems are worthwhile, both to reduce whatever money is being lost and to reassure publics in donor countries at a time when aid budgets are under ever tighter scrutiny.

"... **Domestic economic hardship appears to be resulting in a greater focus on aid budgets. This increases the likelihood that incidents of corruption will lead to calls to cut aid."**
Development Co-operation Report 2010

Aid and corruption – the links

Corruption can strike at almost any point in the chain of relationships between donor and recipient, weakening or destroying the impact of aid. W. Michael Kramer, a US attorney specialising in fraud, has written about some of the ways in which aid can be diverted. One of the most obvious is through bribes: in many cases, he writes, contractors may have to pay a bribe equivalent to between 5% and 20% of the value of the contract they are seeking, and between 2% and 5% of the value of any invoices they submit. Alternatively, they may be asked to provide "gifts" such as funding the education of an official's children or, in one case, providing "free lodging to international aid agency employees". That latter incident is a reminder that corruption can also be found on the donor side of the aid equation. Bid rigging is another aspect of corruption: Qualified and ethically minded contractors may lose out to less scrupulous bidders, even if they offer to do the job for less. Indeed, bid rigging tends to squeeze out cheaper contractors because those who put in a higher bid earn more for doing the same job, and thus have additional funds to pay kickbacks. Corruption can also include outright fraud: a company building an aid-supported road, say, may save money by digging only shallow foundations, and then keep the savings for itself. Or, a supplier may pass off used computers as new equipment, bribing officials to turn a blind eye.

So, the benefits of aid can be weakened by corruption, but can aid itself cause – or even encourage – corruption? It's probably fair to say that most people believe it can: "There are many ways in which aid encourages corruption," says Transparency International. "Where aid has been provided to corrupt systems or under a corrupt leadership, it serves to feed abuses. […]Where aid has undermined domestic accountability mechanisms, it opens up further opportunities for corruption." However, some academic studies have disputed whether aid actually *causes* corruption, arguing instead that in many cases aid simply gets caught up in systems that are already corrupt. One researcher, José Tavares, has even argued that "foreign aid decreases corruption", possibly

CORRUPTION: SUPPLY AND DEMAND

Corruption can be thought of from two perspectives: demand and supply. The **demand side**, which can involve anyone from a government minister demanding money before approving a contract to a policeman who won't let a car pass until a few notes are slipped into his hand. On the other side of the equation is the **supply side** – the foreign firm that pays funds into a minister's overseas bank account or the harassed driver who decides to pay up just to get past the checkpoint.

Most countries have laws covering the demand side, in effect making it an offence to demand or accept bribes, although the extent to which these laws are policed varies greatly. On the supply side, it may also be an offence to offer a bribe. For instance, countries that have signed the **OECD's Anti-Bribery Convention** make it illegal for their domestic firms to pay bribes to foreign officials. Whistle-blowing and education can also play a role in encouraging people not to give in to unreasonable demands. In India, *ipaidabribe.com*, a website set up by an NGO in Bangalore, allows victims of corruption to tell their story, and is helping to change attitudes in government. "If I try to do things on my own here, I may run into rough weather," Bhaskar Rao, a state transport commissioner, told the BBC. "But the evidence on this website gives me some internal support to bring about reforms."

because it "may be associated with rules and conditions that limit the discretion of the recipient country's officials".

Fighting back against corruption

The focus by donors and developing countries on making aid more effective over the past decade or so has included an increased determination to tackle corruption. The issue is referred to explicitly in both the Paris Declaration and in the follow-up declaration, the Accra Agenda for Action, as well as the more recent Busan Partnership for Effective Development Co-operation.

> "Corruption is a plague that seriously undermines development globally… We will intensify our joint efforts to fight corruption and illicit flows… Implement fully our respective commitments to eradicate corruption, enforcing our laws and promoting a culture of zero tolerance for all corrupt practices…"
>
> Busan Partnership for Effective Development Co-operation

As made clear in the Busan statement, this is a question of "mutual accountability" – both developing countries and donors have a role to play. Donors, for example, need to look at corruption in broader contexts: are they policing the OECD Anti-Bribery Convention, which makes it illegal for businesses to pay bribes to foreign officials? Also, are they freezing and recovering illegal assets spirited overseas by officials in developing countries? On the side of the developing country, there is – in the words of the Accra Agenda for Action – a requirement to "address corruption by improving systems of investigation, legal redress, accountability and transparency in the use of public funds". And yet, even though the fight against corruption today is grounded in the principles of aid effectiveness, there's no question that graft can test these to their very limits: "It is difficult to respect partner country leadership that does not appear committed to tackling corruption," as one OECD report states. "It is frustrating to align with partners' anti-corruption strategies where these do not appear to address corruption effectively or show tangible results quickly."

Resolving these tensions is not easy. The response needs to be fine-tuned country-by-country, taking account of unique situations and the inevitable trade-offs between fighting corruption and supporting long-term development. Despite such difficulties, donors have tended to go on engaging with countries even where there are serious concerns about graft. But there are a number of strategies that they have adopted to encourage leaders in developing countries to clamp down on corruption. One is for donors to work together to adopt a common approach: firstly to develop a shared understanding of the scale and the nature of the problem and, secondly, to avoid delivering mixed messages to the developing country's government. In some cases, donors have developed a graduated response to incidents of corruption, and a joint "script" from which they can deliver a unified message. The aim of such approaches is to ensure that the government in the developing country does not try to take advantage of less demanding donors, weakening the overall impact of the anti-corruption effort.

What is policy coherence?

In Malawi, Carlos Varela, a 28-year-old doctor, faced a tough dilemma two years after leaving medical school. He was working at Lilongwe Central Hospital, a clinic with no diagnostic equipment where patients slept two or three to a bed. There was often no point in writing a prescription because the drug cabinet might be bare. For all his efforts, Varela earned just $65 a month. Among the 25 young doctors with whom he graduated, just three were still working in public hospitals in Malawi. Five more were already working abroad or on their way, and they would soon be followed by several others. Dr. Varela, too, was eyeing his options: "I want to stay," he told reporter Stephanie Nolen. "If I leave the government hospital, who's going to work here? But I understand the people who leave – in a few years, I will think about going, too."

The young doctor wasn't the only one facing a dilemma. For his country, the departure of qualified people like Dr. Varela can bring both gains and losses: on the plus side, like most migrants, he would probably send money back home – remittances – which can be a valuable source of funds both for migrants' families and the wider economy. He might also develop new skills and, if he ever came back, these could be good for developing healthcare in Malawi. Against that, there's a chance the doctor may never return, depriving his country of his medical skills, meaning it gets no return for its investment in his training.

For rich donor countries, Dr. Varela's possible departure also presents something of a conundrum. On the one hand, they need well-qualified medical professionals, and that need will only grow as their populations age. On the other hand, recruiting a doctor from a country like Malawi undercuts that country's health system and, in turn, the goal of providing Malawians with decent healthcare. And, domestically, there's the issue of managing migration, a thorny subject in most developed countries. Resolving this puzzle means finding a way to reconcile policy in at least three areas – development, migration and healthcare. In short, policy coherence for development is not easy.

But, easy or not, it's essential if rich and poor countries are to deepen their partnership. Most people now accept that if wealthy countries really want to be partners for development, they need to stretch their thinking well beyond aid to take in a whole range of policy questions – trade, migration, investment and so on. That doesn't mean aid no longer matters – it still does. But it's increasingly regarded as just one part, and in some cases a small part, of a much broader relationship.

"... **Policies ranging from trade and investment to tax and fiscal transparency, corporate governance, climate change, resource security, and social policy have a profound impact on the prospects for achieving sustainable development objectives in a national and global context."**

Angel Gurría, OECD Secretary-General

Some of these themes are addressed explicitly in the **Commitment to Development Index** from the Centre for Global Development, which rates the major donor countries for their policy stances in seven areas – including aid, trade, investment and technology – to determine just how pro-development those policies are. Like any index, it's open to criticism over the choice of issues and how they're balanced one against the other. Nevertheless, it's an interesting – and perhaps provocative – take on how the totality of relationships between rich and poorer countries can shape development prospects.

The challenge of managing these has become even more pressing in the era of globalisation in which we are currently living. The world's economies are becoming ever more interlinked through a series of "flows", typically identified as rising levels of exchange in trade, capital, people and information or technology. The financial crisis and recession of the late 2000s illustrated just how important these flows have become. The collapse of the Lehman Brothers financial services firm sparked immediate fears of a global "contagion" of the world's financial system, while in the months following that event, global trade briefly collapsed too. Such incidents illustrate the reality that countries are no longer able to tackle all the challenges they face on their own, not just in a financial crisis but in areas like climate change. Again, the approaches taken by developed countries, for example regarding carbon emissions, can have grave consequences for poorer countries, and they need to be kept in mind when considering broader policies for development.

Examining every area of policy where the actions of wealthy countries can have an impact on developing countries would take up much of the rest of this book. But looking briefly at one specific issue – trade – may shed some light on the challenges.

Aid for trade

The success of developed and emerging countries like Korea, Japan, China and Mauritius has been driven by many factors, but one stands out in particular – trade. The World Bank's Growth Commission identified trade as one of five key factors in the achievements of the world's "star" economies over the past half century or so. Overall, it's estimated that an increase of 1% in the share of trade in GDP raises national income levels by between 0.9% and 3%.

So, trade matters. But it hasn't been easy for poorer countries to access global markets. For one thing, their goods and services have sometimes faced barriers and unfair competition in developed countries. For another, they haven't always had the capacity to trade effectively in the world economy: bad roads can make it hard to transport goods; ports may not be able to handle cargo vessels; and some countries may not have the technical capacity

6. Changing relationships and policies

WHAT IS AID FOR TRADE?

Aid for trade by region and category
Commitments, 2002-05 and 2009
($ billion, 2009 constant)

Legend:
- Trade-related adjustment
- Trade policy and regulations
- Economic infrastructure
- Building productive capacity

Regions (with '02-'05 Avg and '09 bars): Africa, America, Asia, Europe, Oceania

Source: OECD/WTO (2011), *Aid for Trade at a Glance 2011*.
StatLink: http://dx.doi.org/10.1787/888932606302

WHAT IS AID FOR TRADE?

The idea of using assistance to help developing countries improve their capacity to trade is not new. Indeed, many of the sort of projects that aid has always helped to fund – for example, roads, electricity provision, and even schools – can either directly or indirectly benefit trade, at least over the long term. But in the mid-2000s, the idea was formalised by World Trade Organization ministers, and tied into the Paris Declaration idea of "ownership" – in effect, aid for trade is counted as such only if it ties into the trade-related development priorities of the recipient country.

Aid for trade helps developing countries in a number of ways, For example, building roads and telecoms networks; helping industries and sectors to build on their strengths and diversify their exports; and cushioning the financial pain of adjustment to trade liberalisation measures, such as reducing tariffs. Some of the other ways in which it can help are not, perhaps, so immediately obvious. For instance, international trade negotiations can be extremely complex, requiring high levels of the sort of legal expertise that is not always accessible to developing countries. But aid for trade can be used to help developing countries make up that gap.

Aid for trade now accounts for a large slice of official development assistance (ODA): disbursements have been growing by between 11% and 12% since 2006, and reached $29 billion in 2009. The biggest increase was in aid for trade to Africa, which reached $13 billion, making the continent the largest recipient. This reflects a conscious decision by the development community to focus aid for trade on low-income countries.

to certify that goods they produce pass international health and safety standards.

The importance of overcoming these shortcomings has become increasingly clear in recent years, notably since the launch, in 2001, of the **Doha Development Round** of trade talks, the ninth in a series of international negotiations (dating back to 1947) aimed at boosting global trade. Agreement in this latest round, aimed at integrating developing countries into the global trade system, has however proved elusive, with a number of thorny issues holding up progress, notably disagreements over the support that developed countries give to their own farmers; tariffs on fabric imports; and trade in services, More recently, in 2005, World Trade Organization (WTO) ministers launched an "aid for trade" initiative, with the aim of helping developing countries, especially the least developed, to build up their trade capacity and infrastructure *(see box)*.

Many in the developing world have argued that, although wealthy countries tend to favour trade liberalisation, they don't always do as much as they could to level the trade playing field. For example, in the past OECD countries have been accused of distorting free trade through excessive support for their own farmers, which makes the price of domestically produced goods artificially low and so squeezes out imports from developing countries. According to The Cairns Group, a coalition of 19 agricultural exporting countries that includes developing countries and a number of OECD members, such supports in OECD countries were equivalent to $368 billion a year between 2006 and 2008 – triple their annual ODA totals. Leaders of developing countries argue that such farm support policies are inconsistent with the global drive to increase exports from the developing countries.

In a number of areas barriers to developing countries' exports have been lowered. The European Union's "Everything But Arms" initiative provides duty-free access to its markets to 48 of the world's least developed countries. But in other areas, progress has been frankly disappointing. Most notably, the Doha round of trade talks, which was intended to greatly ease the access of developing countries to global markets in the provision of both goods and services, remains deadlocked – a fact that "bodes ill especially for developing countries," as an OECD report noted recently.

A question of governance

We've looked in this chapter at the idea of deepening the relationship between donors and developing countries. But, as we've seen, for this partnership to work at its best – and for aid to maximise its impact – conditions need to be right in developing countries. They need to be able to manage their own affairs, and their publics need to be involved in the decisions that will affect their lives. In short, they need **good governance**; and that's the subject of the next chapter.

Find Out More

FROM OECD ...

On the Internet

To find out about OECD work on **aid effectiveness**, go to *www.oecd.org/dac/ effectiveness*. The full text of the Busan Partnership for Effective Development Co-operation can be found at *http://www. aideffectiveness.org/busanhlf4* (the full texts of the Paris Declaration and Accra Agenda for Action can be found at *www.oecd.org/ dataoecd/11/41/34428351.pdf*). For work on **policy coherence**, go to *www.oecd.org/ development/policycoherence*, and to learn more about **corruption and development** go to *www.oecd.org/dac/governance/ corruption*.

The OECD hosts an **international platform on policy coherence for development**, which aims to allow "a wide range of stakeholders to share experiences and good practices" in this area: *https://community.oecd.org/ community/pcd*.

The OECD and the World Trade Organisation have created a special website around the **Aid for Trade Initiative** at *www.aid4trade.org*. More information can also be found at *www. oecd.org/dac/aft*.

Publications

Better Aid (series): This series concentrates on the efforts of both donor and recipient countries in realising their Paris Declaration commitments. Titles include *Civil Society and Aid Effectiveness* (2010), which looks at ways to better integrate civil society organisations into development efforts, and *Managing Aid* (2009), which outlines what individual donors are doing to fulfil their commitments under the Paris Declaration and Accra Agenda for Action. Find out more about this series at *www.oecd.org/dac/ publications/betteraid*.

Better Policies for Development – Recommendations for Policy Coherence (2011): This report examines the way in which wider policy tools in areas as diverse as financial regulation, trade and water security can be used to support development objectives, as well at how the OECD is working to integrate its activities more fully into the development co-operation agenda.

Trade for Growth and Poverty Reduction: How Aid for Trade Can Help (2011): This book explains how aid for trade can foster economic growth and reduce poverty, and why it is an important instrument for development strategies that actively support poverty alleviation.

Aid for Trade at a Glance 2011: This joint OECD-WTO publication provides a comprehensive analysis of trends and developments in aid for trade. It offers a positive picture, showing how aid for trade is bettering lives in developing countries. Numerous case stories show the wide variety of trade-related activities in a large number of developing countries that are being supported by a range of donors.

... AND OTHER SOURCES

Transparency International (*www. transparency.org*): Widely regarded as the leading civil society organisation in the fight against corruption; publishes the much-watched Corruption Perceptions Index.

U4 Anti-Corruption Resource Centre (*www.u4.no*): Based in Norway, the centre provides support and services to eight development agencies around the world.

Commitment to Development Index (at *www.cgdev.org*): This Index from the Centre for Global Development looks at whether donor countries' policies in a range of areas are "development friendly".

7

When a country can't run its own affairs, it's the poor who pay the highest price. This is one reason why good governance – including upholding human rights – creating systems of accountability and setting up functioning tax systems have become a major focus of development co-operation.

7. Governance matters

By way of introduction ...

Towards the end of 2010, the people of Côte d'Ivoire went to the polls to elect a new president. After a decade of civil unrest, coups and political instability, the west African country – once considered one of the continent's most stable and prosperous – looked like it might be about to turn a corner. In the run-up to voting day, one Ivorian expressed the hopes of his countrymen: "We are leaving behind lots of things – violence, turmoil, death – and heading to a renaissance," Olivier Coulibaly told the BBC. However, he also sounded a note of caution: "But first we need to pass the dark tunnel."

He could hardly have guessed just how dark that tunnel would be. Despite near-universal praise for how the poll had been handled, the outgoing president, Laurent Gbagbo, refused to accept the result. His decision plunged the country into six months of turmoil, which would claim around a thousand lives, force a million people out of their homes, and lead about 80 000 to seek refuge on the country's borders with Ghana and Liberia. Even after Gbagbo was finally arrested, the legacy of his disastrous decisions would continue to be felt. For 2011, the *African Economic Outlook* warned that the country's economy would contract by over 7% and that its progress in reaching the Millennium Development Goals (MDGs) faced "enormous risks".

The turmoil in Côte d'Ivoire represented an extreme example of the collapse of order in a society. Unfortunately, there are many other cases. Worldwide, 1.5 billion people live in fragile states or areas afflicted by conflict or large-scale, organised criminal violence, according to the most recent edition of The World Bank's *World Development Report*. Such failures are disastrous for development: no low-income fragile state or country afflicted by conflict has attained even one of the MDGs, while people in such countries are more than twice as likely to be undernourished as those in other developing countries. But conflict is only one aspect of a much broader issue facing developing countries – governance. This is about the capacity of countries to govern themselves decently, transparently and accountably. It's also about their ability to create a public space where all citizens, regardless of their backgrounds, can help to shape the decisions that will determine their country's future.

7. Governance matters

▶ In recent decades, the importance of good governance in driving development has been increasingly recognised. This chapter looks, first, at what we mean by governance, and then at a specific aspect of it, namely human rights. It then looks at how concerns over governance have become a major theme in development co-operation and an important influence on how donors "do" aid. In particular, the international community has focused more and more on fragile states, or countries where governance has essentially collapsed. Finally, the chapter looks at how public finances, governance and state accountability can be strengthened in developing countries through improved tax systems.

What is the role of governance?

Governance goes to the heart of whether a society has the capacity to run its own affairs. Where governance is weak, the consequences for economic, social and human development are invariably serious. The similarity between the words *governance* and *government* can be misleading. It's easy to think that governance is just another way of describing what governments do. But it goes deeper than that: governance is not just about the actions taken to run a society's affairs but about *how* these come about. For instance, is a decision taken by a minister behind closed doors, or does it follow a period of consultation with citizens and civil society, with oversight by public representatives and access to information by the media? Governance, then, is about **processes**.

It's also about the **relationship** between the state and the society – the rules that govern the space in which government, citizens, business, civil society, the media and so on can come together to debate challenges and make decisions. Where governance is weak, this space may be closed off to people outside the elites or to specific groups, for instance women or indigenous peoples. The result is that they are denied an opportunity to help shape decisions that may profoundly affect their lives. In this sense, governance is inherently political, meaning that it relates to how societies collectively take decisions.

Definitions like these might be seen as inferring that good governance is synonymous with a particular form of government, most notably the Western democratic model. But this is not necessarily the case. For historical, cultural, social and political reasons, the ways in which societies govern themselves vary greatly, as does the nature of political space. Nevertheless, even if there is no agreement on specific political models, a consensus has grown around the idea that bad governance is bad for development.

So what is good governance? Researchers at the Overseas Development Institute identified six core principles that they argue are now widely accepted in both developing and developed countries as being essential to good governance:

- **Participation:** Do people who are affected by decisions have a say in how they're made?
- **Fairness:** Do the same rules apply equally to everyone?
- **Decency:** Do the rules of society humiliate or harm people or segments of society?
- **Accountability:** Are politicians, officials and other political actors held accountable for what they do?
- **Transparency:** Are decisions made in a clear, open way?
- **Efficiency:** Are human and financial resources put to good use, without waste, delay or corruption?

The role of human rights

Some of these principles relate to governance issues we've already looked at, for example corruption. Others introduce some new ideas, in particular the link between development and human rights, an issue that has risen up the international agenda since the early 1990s. In 1993, for instance, the United Nations stated that "democracy, development and respect for human rights and fundamental freedoms are interdependent and mutually reinforcing …". Four years later, the OECD's Development Assistance Committee (DAC) stated that "respect for human rights is seen as an objective in its own right but also as a critical factor for the longer term sustainability of development activities" (*see also Chapter 1*).

The timing of statements like these in the 1990s is significant. During the Cold War, human rights were highly politicised: countries allied to the West tended to promote civil and political rights; those in the Eastern bloc emphasised economic, social and cultural rights. With the end of the Cold War, some – but not all – of the heat went out of this division. Even today, governments of different political leanings may emphasise one part of the human rights spectrum over another.

How wide is that spectrum? Between 1966 and 1990, the international community adopted seven core treaties on human rights covering a very broad range of issues, including civil and political rights, economic, social and cultural rights, the rights of children and the elimination of racial discrimination and of discrimination against women. By their adoption, the countries of the world accepted that these rights are "universal" – i.e. they apply to every individual. But clearly, in reality, the extent to which rights are respected and recognised varies greatly between countries.

Human rights are not a luxury or legal nicety: as we saw in *Chapter 2*, the absence of such rights forms one aspect of what has come to be called **multidimensional poverty**. The influential South American economist Hernando de Soto has examined the real-world implications of this in the lives of one group of people, the indigenous tribes of the Amazon. De Soto argues that, contrary to romanticised perceptions in the West, indigenous groups want to engage with the global economy to improve their often dire standards of living. Half of Peru's native peoples live in extreme poverty; life expectancy is 20 years below other groups in the country; infant mortality is three times the national average; among children, about one in two suffers from chronic malnutrition.

> "What the people of the Amazon really want is the same thing the poor are seeking throughout the developing world: to be legally empowered so that they are no longer marginalised politically, having a voice in their own economic futures without losing their customs or traditional identities."
>
> Hernando de Soto, *Development Co-operation Report 2011*

The indigenous peoples of the Amazon live in a place of great natural wealth, albeit one that is under severe environmental pressure. But because of a failure to adequately protect their economic rights, they are effectively excluded from taking advantage of their birthright, argues de Soto. Of the 5 000

7. Governance matters

THE ROOTS OF GENDER INEQUALITY

The emphasis on women in the Millennium Development Goals (MDGs) is striking: Goal 3 focuses on gender equality, Goal 5 on the health of mothers and Goal 2 specifically references the need to educate girls (see also Chapter 2). This focus is no accident: for many years, now, the development community has recognised that empowering women to play a full role in social, cultural and economic life benefits not just women but society as a whole.

There is no shortage of evidence: providing girls with just a few years of primary schooling, for example, greatly improves their economic prospects. It also means they are more likely to have fewer, but healthier, children, and to ensure that those children, in turn, attend school. Enhancing the role of women in the economy also brings wider benefits: in Brazil, one study showed that the likelihood of a child's survival rose by 20% when his or her mother controlled household income.

Yet, in many societies, women still continue to experience substantial discrimination, reducing their access to education and depriving them of a voice in national life. Numerous measures exist that allow us to examine these issues, for example the Gender Inequality and Gender Empowerment indices developed by the United Nations Development Programme (UNDP) as companions to its Human Development Index. But a few years ago, the OECD's Development Centre and the University of Göttingen set out to look at the issue in another way, by examining how social norms and institutions shape women's economic and social roles. In effect, rather than examining the "outputs" of discrimination, for example the scarcity in many countries of women with paid jobs, the project examined the causes of such discrimination.

The resulting Social Institutions and Gender (**SIGI**) **Index** focuses on five broad areas of social and legal practice in developing countries, including – among others – the formal and informal rules governing family life, women's ownership rights and violence against women. The research shows up the complex nature of the links between social institutions and, ultimately, development. For example, societies where it's traditional for women to marry young – typically, between 15 and 19, but sometimes even younger – tend to have lower female literacy rates. That, in turn, reduces the size of the talent pool in the workforce, and holds back overall economic development. Understanding such linkages is important to ensuring that development initiatives go some way to addressing the root causes of gender inequality.

Find out more at *http://my.genderindex.org*

indigenous communities in the Peruvian Amazon, only one in twenty has a property title that allows it to control its territory and manage what should be communal resources. The titling process is expensive and arduous – typically, it takes over two years and costs more than $36 000. There have been some reforms, but in most cases property titles are established only within the community and not beyond. The result, argues the economist, is that each community is "imprisoned in its own tiny ghetto, *incommunicado* and unable to co-operate easily in economic terms with people from other communities and beyond". Full recognition of the economic rights of these people would empower them to try to find their own solutions to the poverty that afflicts their communities.

So, human rights go to the heart of economic and social progress. But the link is more complex than it might at first appear. To explain: recognition and implementation of universal human rights can be seen both as a goal and a driver of human development. In other words, progress on human rights in and of itself constitutes development, but also provides a basis for building long-term, sustainable development.

> "Human rights have intrinsic value, and achieving them is seen as an objective in its own right. But human rights are also a critical factor for the long-term sustainability of development."
>
> DAC Action-oriented Paper on Human Rights and Development (2007)

Governance and development co-operation

This fact is increasingly reflected in the way in which development co-operation works and in the approaches of DAC donor governments, which in 1993 committed themselves to developing "clear and credible policies to guide their development co-operation with reference to human rights". Much of this work is carried out under the banner of governance, an area where donor spending rose substantially in the first decade of the new millennium.

The extent to which donors stress governance and human rights issues varies. Some, such as The World Bank, have tended to be reluctant to make explicit references to human rights for fear of being seen as acting politically. Nevertheless, the Bank's work on tackling multidimensional poverty, for example, clearly has a strong human rights dimension. Other donors, such as Sweden, make much more explicit human rights commitments. Poland, which began the transition to democracy as recently as 1989,

7. Governance matters

Strengthening governance
DAC donor spending on strengthening governance, 2002-07
(Current prices, disbursements, in $ millions)

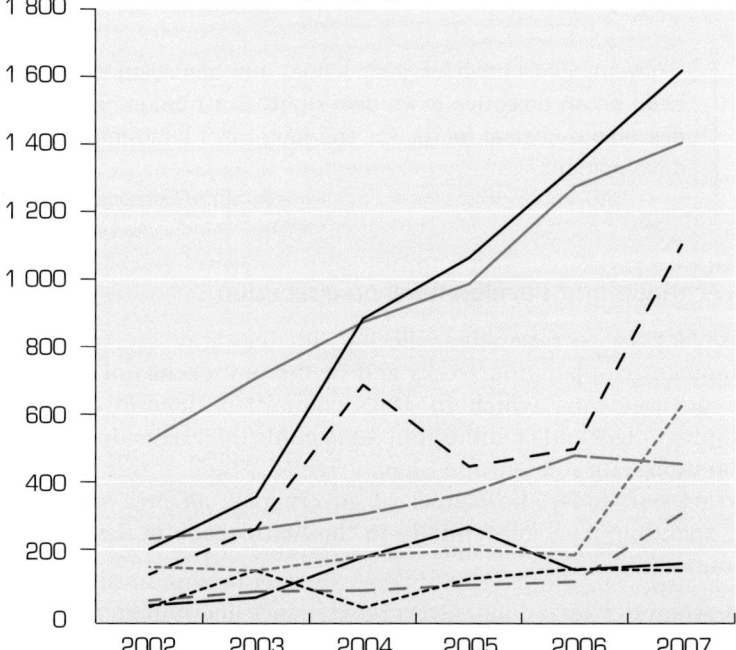

— Economic and development policy/planning
------- Public sector financial management
— — — Legal and judicial development
— Strengthening civil society
——·- Elections
——— Human rights
------- Free flow of information
— — — Women's equality organisations and institutions

Donor spending on a range of governance issues has risen in recent years. There have been notable increases in funding for financial management in the public sector, which is essentially aimed at combating corruption. Support for civil society organisations, which often represent people whose voices may not always be heard in public debate, has also grown.

Source: Development Co-operation Report 2010.
StatLink: http://dx.doi.org/10.1787/888932606321

focuses its bilateral aid on governance and democracy issues where, as an OECD review notes, "it has a comparative advantage".

Donors also pursue human rights and governance issues in many different ways, and can adopt a carrot or stick approach. For example, in 2011, the United Kingdom cut off general budget support for Malawi's government after citing concerns over economic management and governance: "Demonstrations have been suppressed, civil society organisations intimidated, and an Injunctions Bill passed that would make it easier for the Government to place restrictions on opponents without legal challenge," the British government said.

More usually, they seek to be supportive of human rights initiatives and agencies, and at a number of different levels – local projects, national initiatives and global campaigns, for instance. An example of support for a project comes from South Sudan, where Sweden helped to fund a course to educate voters in the run-up to the referendum that established the country in January 2011. One of those who took part of the process was Zainab Osman. Even by going to the polls, she broke a local taboo on women being involved in decision making: "To all of a sudden be able to take part was a wonderful feeling and very emotional for me, as women were not previously allowed to vote in our country," she told Sida, the Swedish aid agency. Donors may also pursue country-wide programmes, such as one by the child-policy agency UNICEF in Viet Nam that began in the mid-1990s with the aim of widening understanding and appreciation of children's rights. The agency adopted a range of approaches, which included providing training for judges, lawyers, police and prison staff, among others, and developing relationships and dialogue with officials at all levels of the government and the Communist Party. And there may be support for global initiatives, such as providing funding for rights-oriented agencies like UNICEF and international non-governmental organisations (NGOs).

Indeed, one of the most common approaches taken by donors is to support civil society groups, which often represent people who may traditionally be excluded from economic and political life. In Ghana, for example, funding from the United Kingdom helped an association of market women to lobby for better working conditions and allowed them to get training in book-keeping. For years, the women had dreaded the arrival of tax officials, who often made demands that were unrelated to the women's incomes and offered confusing advice. But once they had learned how to keep their books, the women could show their profits at the end of the month, and could be taxed fairly. "My business and that of other women in the market is better because we spoke up and took action about our concerns," Cynthia Mensah, the head of the market women's group told DFID, the UK Department for International Development. "Some of us are expanding our business and with stable incomes we are also now in the position to provide for our families."

> "Integrating human rights into development co-operation can ... help to achieve more effective poverty reduction and social outcomes."
>
> *Integrating Human Rights and Development (2006)*

This story illustrates well the dual linkage between human rights and development discussed earlier: empowering women economically is an important part of ensuring gender equality. But it also provides a basis for further development, in this case the expansion of the women's businesses and the additional funds that help to feed and educate their families. Similar examples abound, as do development initiatives targeted specifically at groups that suffer social or economic exclusion, for instance indigenous peoples, homosexuals, people with disabilities and children who have slipped through the cracks of society.

The increasing focus on human rights in development policy reflects just one way in which the importance of governance is now recognised. In the next section, we'll examine another important strand in the governance story – supporting and strengthening fragile states.

What are fragile states?

State fragility threatens the lives and livelihoods of up to 1.5 billion people in some 30-40 countries. People in such countries are more than twice as likely to be undernourished as those in other developing countries, and more than twice as likely to lack clean water. For the OECD, "fragile states" are those that have poor capacity to carry out the basic functions of governing

> **DAC PRINCIPLES ON HUMAN RIGHTS AND DEVELOPMENT**
>
> In 2007, the OECD's Development Assistance Committee identified ten principles aimed at strengthening the link between human rights and development co-operation. The principles cover a lot of ground, and some of the ideas may be a little hard to grasp for non-specialists. For instance, one key theme is the idea of linking human rights with the principles of aid effectiveness (see Chapter 6). What this can mean in practice, for example, is ensuring that the "ownership" of a country's development agenda is not solely in the hands of a governing elite, but instead reflects the needs and interests of as much of society as possible, especially those whose lives are going to be affected by development initiatives.
>
> Other ideas in the principles are more obvious, such as "Do no harm", reminding donors that their actions in developing countries can be both beneficial and harmful. "If issues of faith, ethnicity and gender are not taken fully into consideration," the principles note, "they can inadvertently reinforce societal divisions, worsen corruption, exacerbate violent conflict, and damage fragile political coalitions."
>
> Find out more at www.oecd.org/dataoecd/50/7/39350774.pdf

their populations and its territories, and that lack the ability to develop mutually constructive and mutually reinforcing relations with society. As a consequence, trust and mutual obligations between the state and its citizens have become weak.

What does this mean in practice? It means that children may not be able to go to school because of fear of being attacked and that the only people who'll protect you from an armed gang are the members of another armed gang. You may live in a country with a wealth of natural resources, but you are poor and unemployed. Most teachers, doctors and judges have fled abroad. Your country receives lots of international assistance, but the results are nowhere to be seen. For a government trying to deal with problems like these after years of conflict, and trying to figure out the most urgent priority, the MDGs remain the ultimate objectives. But, as we've seen, not a single low-income fragile state is likely to achieve any of them soon.

At the Second Global meeting of the International Dialogue on Peacebuilding and Statebuilding in the Liberian capital Monrovia in June 2011, representatives from over 40 countries, international organisations and civil society groups called for a "New Deal for international development co-operation in conflict-affected and fragile countries". The delegates agreed that peace-building and state-building objectives are a prerequisite to reach the MDGs in fragile states and states affected by conflict. They exchanged experiences on what has worked, what hasn't, and what different partners should do to "move from fragility to agility", as the Liberian minister for planning and economic affairs, Amara Konneh, put it. National and international partners agreed on the "Monrovia Roadmap", which outlines five objectives for peace-building and state-building and a set of practical steps to work towards them. These include establishing targets and indicators to monitor progress towards the objectives, strengthening national leadership for peace-building, and lifting obstacles to effective international assistance.

Five objectives

The 2011 *World Development Report* describes how the nature of conflict has changed. Since the 1980s, the incidence of war between states has declined, and deaths from civil wars are now a quarter of what they were. But other forms of violence and crime have become worse, due to domestic and international stresses such as youth unemployment, income shocks, tensions among ethnic, religious or social groups, and trafficking networks. **Establish and strengthen citizen security** is therefore one of the five newly agreed objectives. Without security and the assurance that people can go about their daily lives in safety, the rest is meaningless.

But who should implement objectives, and monitor progress? If the state hasn't functioned for years or is seen as defending special interests, then conflict resolution and other political processes have to start by building trust among groups who may be hostile to each other. The Roadmap calls on states to **foster inclusive political settlements and conflict resolution**. It can be hard for governments to see civil society as a partner, but an accountable government has a better chance of resolving conflicts and stopping them arising in the first place.

Peace is unlikely to last long if feelings of injustice persist, so it's vital, says the Roadmap, to **address injustices and support increasing citizen access to justice**. This illustrates the practical implications of expressions like "capacity building". Judges, lawyers and other legal professionals need to be trained, but many societies also have non-formal systems for administering justice, and it's worth exploring the possibility of using these where appropriate.

Unemployment is a source of tension and can fuel conflict. For many young men, joining an armed group may be the most attractive job available, or the only one, if they want to feed their family. A Somali pirate for instance can earn from $12 000 to $150 000 from a successful hijack according to a report in the *Financial Times*, compared with $500 a year for the average Somali citizen. The objective to **generate employment and improve livelihoods** highlights the fact that in fragile states, employment creation will require a mix of labour-intensive public and community works, increased agricultural productivity, and domestic private sector development.

All this costs money, and although international partners will continue to finance some activities (fragile states receive over 30% of official development assistance, or ODA), the objective is to **manage revenues and build capacity** for accountable and equitable social service delivery. It's an ambitious set of objectives, but as Liberian President Ellen Johnson Sirleaf pointed out at the Monrovia meeting, "The challenges are huge, but they're no bigger than challenges we've faced in the past".

How can taxation help development?

The challenge of meeting the MDGs is substantial, both logistically and financially. If Sub-Saharan Africa is to reach the goal of universal primary education, for example, it will need to find an extra 3.8 million teachers by 2015, according to UNESCO. To meet all eight MDGs and improve infrastructure, Africa as a whole would need an estimated annual investment of $93 billion in the first five years of this decade.

Aid from the traditional donors in the developed world can help, but on its own it won't be enough. As we've seen, it has been joined in recent years by substantial sources of aid from new donors (*see also Chapter 8*). And there have been increasing flows from private sources, too, including business investment and remittances from emigrants. But even all this won't be enough. To meet their goals, developing countries will need to continue developing their own domestic funding. These come from several sources: on one side, there are **private sources** – essentially, the money that people put into bank accounts, rather than under their mattress, and which banks can then lend to things like businesses and entrepreneurs.

7. Governance matters

On the other, there are **public sources**: these include bonds issued by governments, revenues which can generate things like infrastructure, including roads and schools. But there's another domestic source of revenue that's been gaining increasing interest in recent years – taxation.

> "... Taxation is increasingly seen as one of the key building blocks for development and the main way by which developing countries can mobilise their domestic resources to build their own futures and to reduce their reliance on aid."
>
> Jeffrey Owens, *The OECD's Current Tax Agenda April 2011*

The benefits of tax

It may be a surprise to some, but throughout the developing world, tax is already a much bigger source of finance than aid. Take Africa: on average, Africa collected $441 in tax per person in 2008, but received aid equivalent to just $41 per person. That, of course, was an average for an entire continent, and there were exceptions, but perhaps surprisingly few: aid exceeded tax revenues in only one quarter of the 48 countries for which data was available.

So, just as in developed countries, tax is already a meaningful source of finance for developing countries. But there are differences: the tax take in developing countries tends to be proportionally lower than in the OECD area. In half of Sub-Saharan African countries, it stands at below 15% of GDP compared to about 35% in OECD countries. And it tends to be more narrowly based: in much of Africa, for instance, the bulk of tax comes from the exploitation of natural resources, such as minerals and oil extraction, and a much smaller share from income and property taxes. In political terms, these sorts of taxes are often easier to manage than the likes of corporate and personal income taxes and sales taxes. But that narrow focus comes at a price: if, for instance, oil producers suddenly reduce production for any reason, the government's tax revenues may collapse.

Broadening the mix of taxes reduces the risk of such sudden changes, but it also helps to ensure taxes fulfil their role of tying together the diverse interests of society. As US President F.D. Roosevelt once said, "Taxes ... are the dues that we pay for the privileges of membership in an organized society." Those privileges include the right to hold government accountable for its actions, a right that's reinforced when the government is spending citizens' – and not donors' – money.

The role of taxation in state-building and strengthening governance has attracted deepening interest over the past decade, and is the subject of extensive research. Some of this work has drawn parallels with how tax collection evolved in Western Europe and North America. Although taxation can be traced back to at least the time of the pharaohs, the modern system began to take shape in Western Europe in the 1600s. Facing the constant threat of warfare, rulers in countries like Britain and the Netherlands sought ways to raise revenues. While tax collection in previous eras had often relied on the threat of force, the European monarchs found it easier to negotiate with wealthy holders of capital. This had two consequences: firstly, these elites demanded greater political representation and a greater role in how the state was run. Secondly, to collect tax revenues, states had to develop professional bureaucracies. It's worth remembering that these processes took place over many centuries; by contrast, many developing countries are trying to develop sustainable tax systems in just a few decades.

> "... The need to raise taxation can strengthen state-society relationships with positive consequences for state capacity and the extent to which governments are responsive and accountable to their citizens."
>
> Citizen-State Relations: Improving Governance through Tax Reform (2010)

The links between tax and state-building are complex, but they can be thought of through these three processes:

> **Developing a shared interest in economic growth:** Governments that depend on taxes depend in turn on the prosperity of taxpayers – if taxpayers have no money, they can't pay tax. So, a strong and broad tax system creates incentives for governments to promote economic growth and not, for example, to rely on revenues from aid, corrupt practices or non-sustainable income from natural resources.

> **Developing the state's tools:** States that rely on taxes, and especially direct taxes like income tax, need to develop an adequate bureaucracy for tax collection. This can lay the ground for broader improvements in public administration.

> **Developing accountability and responsiveness**: Taxation engages citizens collectively in politics and leads them to make claims on government. In turn, governments must respond to these demands to enhance tax compliance and sustain state revenues.

The importance of these linkages is underlined by thinking of the situation in reverse – what happens in states that are *not* reliant on tax revenue? An extreme case is the "resource curse" – governments that rely on natural resources, such as oil, for all their revenues. Although there are worthy exceptions, such as Botswana, many resource-rich states share similar troubling characteristics: for example, because governments are independent of taxpayers, they have no need to respond to their interests; in turn, citizen-taxpayers have no real leverage over government. Governments may also use their reserves to pay off the opposition, or to fund repressive internal security. Also, as long as the oil money is flowing, there's no real incentive for government to promote wider economic growth, or to try to bring wealth to remote regions that lack resources.

"… **Large oil and mineral revenues are associated with low levels of democracy and states unbound by law."**
Governance, Taxation and Accountability: Issues and Practices (2008)

It's sometimes argued that aid can cause similar problems, creating in effect an "aid curse": the theory goes that if governments are **aid dependent**, they have less need to develop their own domestic sources of revenue such as income taxes and may, in turn, be less accountable to their own citizens. They may also be more inclined to serve the interests and concerns of their donors, not their citizens. Does this actually happen in practice? The question is hotly debated in development circles, and the evidence is not conclusive one way or the other. Nevertheless, the issue is one of concern, both for governments in developing countries and donors. Improving standards of governance is a task for leaders in each developing country. But donors do have a role to play to ensure they don't exacerbate any problems, for example by making excessive demands on recipient governments or providing them with an excuse not to listen to parliament or representatives of civil society.

Barriers to tax collection

Before improving tax flows becomes a reality, many developing countries may need to overcome a number of obstacles. One is the lack of adequate systems and resources for tax collection. Another is the fact that people in developing countries may be wary of paying taxes, because they fear their money will be wasted or stolen. There are solid grounds for such concerns: in many of the world's poorest countries, relatively large sums of money go abroad without being accounted for. Between 1990 and 2008, illegal cross-border financial flows were equivalent on average to about 4.8% of GDP in 48 of the world's least developed countries, according to a UNDP study. In some countries they were much higher – in Chad, they were estimated at over 27% of GDP. Annually, global cross-border flows of proceeds from criminal activities, corruption, and tax evasion are typically put at between $1 trillion and $1.6 trillion. The extent of these flows makes for a strange paradox: although Africa relies heavily on foreign financing, it actually sends more money abroad than it takes in.

These illicit flows are linked to tax in two ways. First, taxes paid by citizens in some countries undoubtedly get caught up in corrupt practices and are funnelled abroad by politicians or bureaucrats. Second, and on a much larger scale, there is tax evasion and tax avoidance – worldwide phenomena that deprive societies in both developed and developing countries of financing. This isn't just a matter of domestic taxpayers managing to avoid paying their dues. Among the main offenders are multinational companies that typically have operations in dozens of countries, forming what is in effect large internal economies. When money, goods or services are exchanged between separate parts of a multinational, they are accounted for through **transfer pricing** – a highly technical process that's prone to abuse. For example, a multinational may declare its losses in countries where it actually makes or sells its goods, and its profits in a low-tax jurisdiction where it has little more than a

7. Governance matters

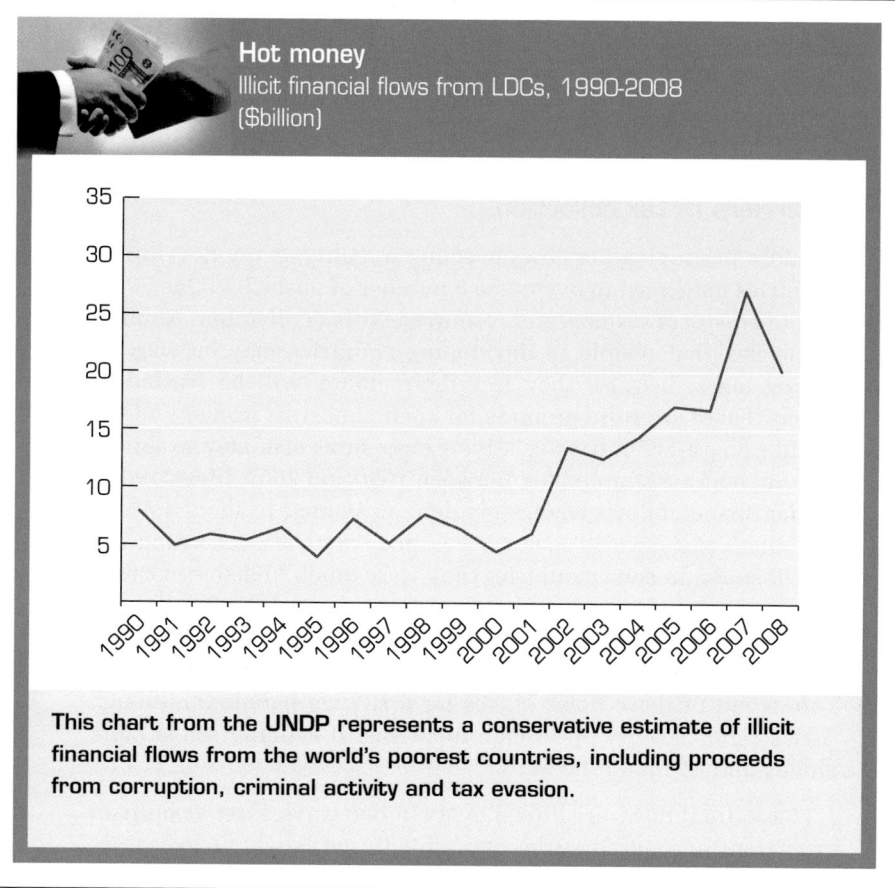

Hot money
Illicit financial flows from LDCs, 1990-2008 ($billion)

This chart from the UNDP represents a conservative estimate of illicit financial flows from the world's poorest countries, including proceeds from corruption, criminal activity and tax evasion.

Source: UNDP (2011), *Illicit Financial Flows from the Least Developed Countries: 1990–2008*.

legal presence. Is this kind of practice illegal? Often not – it may represent tax *avoidance*, or legal actions aimed at reducing a tax bill, and not tax *evasion*, which is illegal.

But the line between evasion and avoidance can be fine; equally, just because a tax practice is legal – at least technically – it doesn't necessarily mean it should be. Indeed, in the wake of the financial crisis, leaders of the G20 group of developed and emerging economies adopted a much tougher stance on tax abuses, declaring that they stood ready "to deploy sanctions to protect our public finances and financial systems". Since then, long-standing work by the OECD to clamp down on tax havens has been stepped up, and there's also been growing pressure for rules and guidelines to be applied more consistently worldwide to reduce tax loopholes and illegal financial flows. But more needs to be done, and many of the steps that need to be taken will require concerted international action. In the context of development co-operation, these efforts can be seen as tied to the idea of **policy coherence** *(see Chapter 6)*. The policy approaches of both developed and developing countries need to tackle financial abuses with the aim of supporting, not undercutting, the bigger project of driving development.

Tax and aid

International effort is also needed to help developing countries improve their tax-collection capabilities. This is not just a case of developing an efficient bureaucracy, although that's certainly important; taxation is a complex issue, and how a tax system is designed can have a huge economic impact. To some extent, there's a "sweet spot" in levying taxes – make them too high, and you suck money out of the economy and encourage people to avoid or evade paying their taxes; make them too low, and the revenues are barely worth the effort of collecting them. Getting the balance right requires expertise, and developed countries can help to provide that as well as offering necessary funding. Currently, though, this sort of work attracts less than 0.1% of ODA. That could certainly be raised.

However, the tax effort goes beyond aid: many of the success stories in improving tax systems come from situations where developing countries are working with each other. In Africa, the African Tax Administration Forum, which is supported by bodies like the OECD and the African Development Bank, brings together more than 30 countries to promote effective tax administration. It provides a place for African countries to learn from each other's experiences, which are likely to be far more relevant than those of developed countries. For example, in Ghana, traditional chiefs retain enormous influence in society, and their agreement can be crucial to the success of the central government's policies. Understanding their influence, and working with them, has been crucial to making effective tax reforms.

WHAT IS THE TASK FORCE ON TAX AND DEVELOPMENT?

In 2010, the OECD set up a group called the **Informal Task Force on Tax and Development** to focus on helping developing countries make the most of taxation to fund development.

Co-chaired by the Netherlands and South Africa, it brings together NGOs, business and other international organisations.

The group focuses on four issues: aid effectiveness, transparency in financial reporting, transfer pricing and international exchange of tax and financial information.

A wider development effort

Strengthening tax systems can be seen both as a tool to improve governance and a source of new funds for development. In the next, and final chapter, of this book, we'll look at another relatively new source of funds and ideas for development – the world's newly emerging economies.

Find Out More

FROM OECD ...

On the Internet

For an introduction to OECD work on **governance** and development, go to *www.oecd.org/dac/governance*, where there's also a link to work on **taxation and governance** (see also the OECD's Centre for Tax Policy and Administration at *www.oecd.org/ctp*). To find out more about work on **conflict areas** and **fragile states**, go to *www.oecd.org/dac/conflict*; for information on the **Fragile States Principles** and their monitoring, go to *www.oecd.org/fsprinciples*. Information on **capacity development** is available at *www.oecd.org/dac/capacitydevelopment*.

Details of work on **gender** and development issues can be found at *www.oecd.org/dac/gender*, while the Social Institutions and Gender Index (SIGI) can be accessed at *http://my.genderindex.org/*; also of interest is *www.wikigender.org*, a project initiated by the OECD's Development Centre to improve knowledge of gender equality-related issues around the world.

Publications

Integrating Human Rights into Development: Donor Approaches, Experiences and Challenges (2006): This book seeks to enhance understanding on the need to work more strategically and coherently on the integration of human rights and development. It reviews the approaches and rationales of donor agencies, and identifies current practice.

Conflict and Fragility (series): This series of books looks at issues of violent conflict and fragile governments in developing countries, and how aid can be designed to reduce violence and strengthen governments. Titles include *Supporting Statebuilding in Situations of Conflict and Fragility* (2011), which offers advice on how donors can help to strengthen the foundations upon which capable, accountable and responsive states are built, and *Do No Harm* (2009), which offers advice to donors on avoiding inadvertently undermining the processes of statebuilding.

Citizen-State Relations: Improving Governance Through Tax Reform (2010): This book sets out to translate research into a practical agenda for action for governments of developing countries and donors. Including numerous real-world examples, it shows how those governments, with the support by donors, can strengthen the state building role of taxation.

African Economic Outlook 2010: This edition includes a special section focusing on mobilisation of public resources, including tax collection, in Africa.

... AND OTHER SOURCES

World Development Report 2011 (The World Bank): This edition of the annual report "examines the changing nature of violence in the 21st century, and underlines the negative impact of repeated cycles of violence on a country or region's development prospects."

World Governance Indicators (*http://info.worldbank.org/governance/wgi/index.asp*): This World Bank project examines six dimensions of governance for most of the world's countries.

The Ibrahim Index (*www.moibrahimfoundation.org*): Produced annually by the Mo Ibrahim Foundation, this sets out to examine the quality of governance across African countries.

8

As it's done before, the global economy is shifting once again, with the emergence of new economic powerhouses like China and India. They're becoming important partners for the world's poorest countries, introducing new ideas, energy and money, but also new challenges for development co-operation.

New partners for development

8. New partners for development

By way of introduction ...

Liu Hui was already in his mid-30s when he took his first trip outside China. He was a reluctant traveller. Leaving China meant saying goodbye to his wife and seven-year-old son. It also meant going to a country he knew little about, Kenya. "My image was: very poor, dry and hot," Liu told Xan Rice of *The Guardian* newspaper. "But if my company wanted to send me somewhere, what could I have done?"

Liu's journey has lasted more than six years, and has involved him in two major construction projects – the upgrading of Nairobi's main airport and the construction of a highway to a fruit-growing area in Kenya's northeast. He's one of about 100 Chinese on the road project. The other workers are locals, and cultural differences between the two groups can make for difficulties. "Chinese work very hard, very quickly, says the civil engineer. "But here we are training local people to do the work, and if someone does not understand, he works slowly. You have to watch."

Liu represents the human face of China's fast-growing engagement with Africa. Estimates vary, but there are now perhaps a million Chinese in Africa. Many are engineers, like Liu, others are labourers working in the heat of the African sun. There are also medical workers, managers in import-export firms, roadside traders, cooks, and many, many more. China's engagement in Africa is not uncontroversial: "China is taking the place of the West: they take our raw materials and they sell finished goods to the world," one Congolese lawyer told *The Atlantic* magazine. Others take a more benign view: "The Chinese bring what Africa needs: investment and money for governments and companies," Rwanda's President Paul Kagame has stated.

However you view it, there's no doubt that the rising involvement of emerging economies like China, India and Brazil is creating a new dynamic in the global economy and in development co-operation, building links between the countries of "the South" that bypass the traditional economic powers in Europe and North America. That's adding a new dimension to the global development picture. But it's also providing new opportunities for developing countries. Harnessing those opportunities, and ensuring that they bring benefits to the world's poorest people, will be an important challenge.

8. New partners for development

▶ This chapter looks at **South-South co-operation**. It begins by examining the context for the rise in South-South linkages, namely the rapid economic emergence of giants like China, India and Brazil. It then looks at the impact of South-South development co-operation, especially the role of China in Africa, and at the emergence of "triangular co-operation," involving traditional donors, emerging economies and developing countries.

How is the world shifting?

In the second half of the 13th century, the young Venetian merchant Marco Polo left Venice and began a series of journeys that would take him away from his home for decades. Historians have long debated Polo's claims, but if what he said was true, the merchant travelled all the way from Venice to Singapore on treks that took him through the Middle East, Central Asia and much of China.

Polo's tales made him famous even in his own lifetime, and may have earned him the nickname "Il Milione". Some say that was a reference to the million lies he supposedly told; others, that it referred to his use of the unfamiliar word "million" to describe the great wealth he saw in China. In his tales, he speaks of Suju (probably present-day Suzhou), "a very great and noble city" whose people "possess silk in great quantities, from which they make gold brocade and other stuffs, and they live by their manufactures and trade". And, long before the innovation caught on in Europe, he describes paper money with which people "can buy what they like anywhere over the Empire".

How much of it is true? No one knows for sure. But even if Polo embroidered the truth, the fact that he thought China wealthy shouldn't be a great surprise. According to estimates by the economic historian Angus Maddison, average wealth per person in China was marginally higher than in Europe at the time of Polo's odyssey, a situation that only began to reverse in the century after Polo returned home. There's an important qualifier in that last sentence – *marginally*. At the time, the wealth gap between China and Europe, or between almost anywhere on the planet, wasn't all that great.

In fact, the huge inequalities we know today – especially those between developed and developing countries – emerged only

OECD Insights: From Aid to Development 149

8. New partners for development

> ### WHO WAS ANGUS MADDISON?
>
> Much economic discussion is concerned with fairly immediate questions: did inflation fall in the last quarter, will unemployment rise in the next? In *The World Economy A Millennial Perspective* the economic historian Angus Maddison (1926-2010) took things much, much further. In this remarkable study for the OECD Development Centre, Maddison traced the contours of the global economy over a thousand years, "trying to explain why some countries achieved faster growth or higher income levels than others".
>
> In a second volume, *Chinese Economic Performance in the Long Run*, Maddison examined the tangled economic history of China from 960 AD to modern times, and demonstrated, as *The New York Times* noted in his obituary, "that China's recent rise was merely a return to economic superpowerdom, as the Middle Kingdom had already dominated the world economy for many centuries."

relatively recently in human history. According to Maddison's estimates, in the year 1000, wealth per person (or GDP per capita) in Europe was actually marginally lower than in Africa, $400 compared with $416. Even 200 hundred years ago, the average European was only about three times better off than his African counterpart. But by the end of the 20th century, all had changed: the average person in Western Europe was 13 times wealthier than in Africa, with GDP per capita of $17 921 compared with $1 368. The figures at the extreme end are even more striking: according to International Monetary Fund (IMF) estimates for 2010, GDP per person in Burundi stood at just over $177; in Luxembourg, it was over $104 000, or more than 580 times higher.

What happened? Economic historians debate this question endlessly, but it's perhaps enough to say that the world economy began to change profoundly in the early 19th century. Technological innovation, industrialisation, urbanisation, and colonisation allowed economies in Western Europe and North America to take off, albeit often at the expense of those living in their overseas colonies. Progress was rapid and striking, even to those living through it: "It is impossible to contemplate the progress of manufactures in Great Britain within the last 30 years without wonder and astonishment," a Scottish merchant, Patrick Colquhoun, wrote in 1814. That period of rapid change helped lay the foundations for much of the world economic order throughout the 20th century, one where it was possible to speak of a split between a relatively well-off "North" and a struggling "South".

The world shifts again

Now, as in Mr. Colquhoun's time, we are again in a time of transition. And, just as in Marco Polo's era, we can read wondrous stories from the East: "Welcome to Chongqing," declares *Foreign Policy* magazine, a little breathlessly, "the biggest city you've never heard of." Chongqing, a flourishing city on China's Yangtze river, is as good a symbol as any of the rapid change that is reshaping the world's economic geography. Home to just two million people in the late 1960s, it now has a population of 32 million and is "growing so quickly its maps are already out of date by the time they are printed," says the magazine. Land is scarce, and Chongqing's high-rises are built so close together that people say when you want to borrow money, "you can simply lean out the window of one skyscraper and grab an envelope from someone's extended hand the next skyscraper over." A tall tale, literally.

> "The year 1990 proved to be the midpoint of a cluster of major events that would reshape the world both politically and economically."
>
> *Perspectives on Global Development 2010*

Much of the transition in the world economy that Chongqing represents began to get under way in the early 1990s following a series of global political events: China's leadership decided to step up the pace of economic reforms that had begun in the late 1970s; India elected a new, pro-reform government; and the Iron Curtain that had separated Europe since shortly after World War II came down. The result was to bring developing countries like China and India and regions like the former Soviet bloc more fully into the global economy. In just a few years in the 1990s, the global market for goods is estimated to have increased by 2.5 billion people while the total labour force grew by 1.5 billion. Around about the same time, global barriers to flows of capital and investment and to trade were sharply reduced, allowing the emerging economies to take full advantage of established and newly created markets. In effect, this marked the beginning of a new phase of economic globalisation, the first since the early 20th century.

8. New partners for development

The emergence of these economies gained a firm foothold in the first decade of the new millennium, creating a phenomenon that the OECD Development Centre refers to as "shifting wealth" – a redirecting of the world's economic gravity away from the traditional economic powerhouses of the OECD area and towards emerging economies like China and India. The figures are striking: in 1990, OECD countries accounted for 62% of the world economy; by 2030, that share is forecast to fall to 43%, with the remainder, or 57%, accounted for by emerging and developing countries. But we don't need to look to the future to get a sense of this shift: in 2008, just as the economic crisis began to hit, GDP in developing countries grew by 5.6% compared with just 0.5% in the developed countries of the OECD. For the foreseeable future, emerging and developing countries look set to continue growing at a much stronger pace than their developed counterparts.

Those numbers need a little further explanation, for several reasons. Firstly, countries that are economically behind can often notch up a much faster pace of growth than their wealthier counterparts and still remain relatively poor. Take China and Japan: China has regularly enjoyed annual growth of at least 8% since the 1990s, sometimes touching 11%, whereas Japan has rarely seen growth in excess of 3% and has suffered through several periods of economic contraction. Yet, as we saw in *Chapter 2*, GDP per capita in Japan is still ten times higher than in China.

Secondly, lumping all developing countries into one category can be misleading. It's true that many developing countries have seen relatively strong growth in recent years – in 2007, just as the financial crisis hit, 84 developing countries were experiencing growth in per capita income that was at least double that of OECD countries. But many of these will struggle to maintain that growth over the long term. There's no shortage of countries that have enjoyed growth spurts, but, as an OECD report notes, "only rarely are they sustained over long periods".

Nevertheless, the impact of the remarkable shift that the world economy has seen over the past couple of decades is already having profound effects on all our lives. It's also helping to reshape the global development agenda, providing a new source of funding, ideas and development partnerships.

WHAT CAN AFRICA LEARN FROM CHINA?

The economic transformation of China clearly begs a question for other developing countries: can we do it too? That question is one of many that have been looked at by the China-DAC Study Group, a grouping of experts from the OECD's Development Assistance Committee and the International Poverty Reduction Centre in China, which set out to examine whether lessons from China can be applied in Africa.

One of the most important factors identified by the group was China's creation in the late 1970s of a "national project" to go from poverty to middle-income status within a generation. This committed the state to a clear course of action, but allowed room for bottom-up initiatives at everything from provincial to village level. China thus exercised ownership of its development project, but dispersed it widely. That ownership was evident in how China dealt with donors. Instead of seeing aid as a continuing revenue stream, it used aid and investment to acquire know-how and management skills to modernise the economy. Indeed, knowledge was another key part of China's development, with heavy investment in education and research.

Another key was pragmatism. China stuck with what worked and dropped what didn't – an approach that Deng Xiaoping, who led the country's transformation, is said to have described as "crossing the river by feeling the stones". In agriculture, early successes in replacing collectivisation with family ownership of farms were replicated nationwide, providing a basis for greatly increased agricultural output. In industry, China experimented first with developing an export-led sector in a Special Economic Zone in Shenzhen, southern China, before applying lessons learnt more widely. And, despite remaining officially a communist state, China took an essentially non-ideological approach to the roles of the state and the market in the economy, utilising the strengths of both.

There are negative lessons to be learnt, too: China's rapid growth has come at a high environmental cost, and there are widening wealth divisions, especially between urban and rural areas. To continue growing, China also now faces the challenge of moving beyond labour-intensive manufacturing and into higher-end industries.

Few would doubt that China's experience can offer useful lessons for other developing countries, most notably the ownership that it exercised over its own development programme and its success in developing local know-how. But, equally, such lessons need to be adapted to countries' unique local circumstances. As Deng Xiaoping once told a visiting African president, "Please don't copy our model. If there is any experience on our part, it is to formulate policies in light of one's own national conditions."

8. New partners for development

What is South-South co-operation?

"China has provided the largest amounts of financial and technical assistance among the developing countries over the past thirty years …". Sounds contemporary? In fact, this quote from an OECD report dates from 1985, more than a quarter of a century ago. The involvement of emerging economies like China and India in Africa and South America is often described as "new," but these countries have long had substantial official and unofficial engagement with other developing countries. In China's case, they stretch back more than six decades, while India's programme dates back to independence in 1947. What has changed – and what perhaps justifies the title of this chapter – is the scale of their engagement, not just in terms of aid initiatives but across a wide swathe of economic life.

For example, the Indian multinational Tata, which produces almost everything from steel to coffee, is now the second-most active investor in Sub-Saharan Africa. Meanwhile China is now the leading trading partner of Brazil, South Africa and India. Some numbers also illustrate the point: over a decade that saw a substantial rise in Africa's trade – it more than doubled from $247 billion in 2000 to $629 billion in 2009 – the emerging economies claimed an increasing slice of the action. At the start of the decade, Africa's "traditional" partners, mainly North America and Europe, accounted for 77% of the continent's trade (Africa's imports and exports); by 2009, their share had slipped to 61.5%. Over the same period, the "emerging" partners' share grew from 23% to 38.5%. The rise was especially notable for China, which saw its share of Africa's trade almost triple from 4.7% to 13.9%, but India also put in a strong performance, more than doubling its share from 2.3% to 5.1%.

The change has probably been less dramatic when it comes to investment, with the traditional partners appearing to retain the lion's share (it's difficult to come up with exact numbers as reliable data is absent for many African countries). However, estimates from a study of 11 African countries suggest that here, too, emerging economies are playing a bigger role, with their share of foreign direct investment, or FDI, almost doubling from 5.6% in the first half of the 2000s to 10.2% in the second half; among them, India saw its share more than quadruple from 0.4% to 1.7%.

So, there is a clear and emerging picture of much greater economic engagement between the emerging economies and Africa, but also with other parts of the world, such as Latin America. There is also plenty of evidence of increasing efforts in development co-operation by the emerging economies – a phenomenon that is attracting increasing attention. And, just as the efforts of traditional donors come under occasional attack, the involvement of the "new" partners, too, has not gone without its share of criticism.

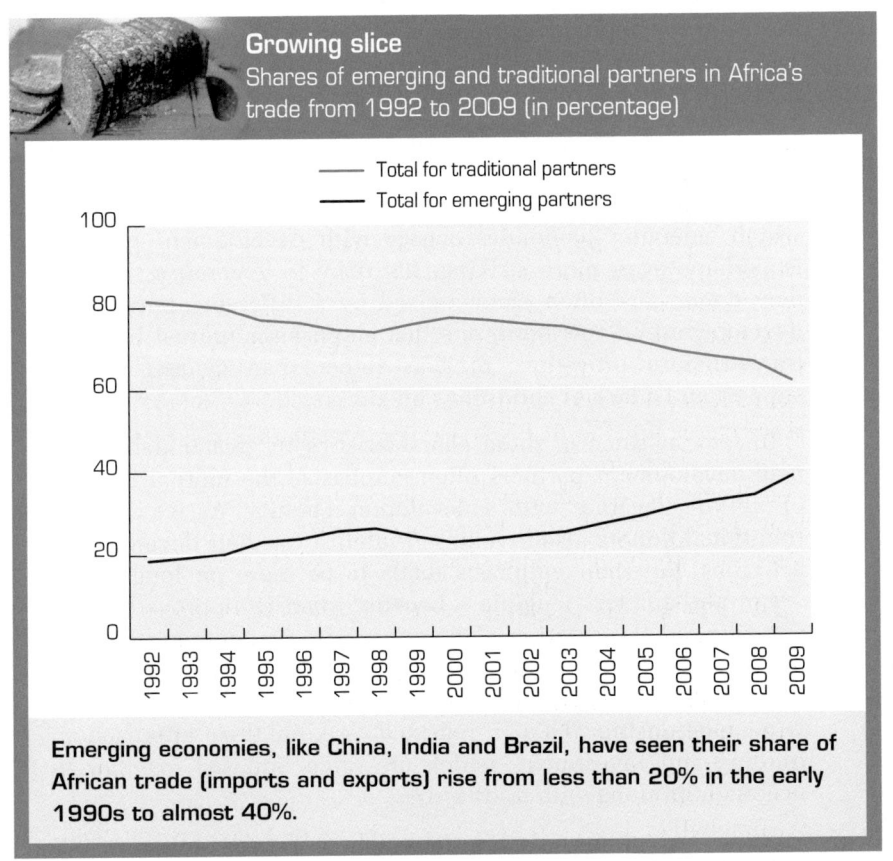

Growing slice
Shares of emerging and traditional partners in Africa's trade from 1992 to 2009 (in percentage)

Emerging economies, like China, India and Brazil, have seen their share of African trade (imports and exports) rise from less than 20% in the early 1990s to almost 40%.

Source: OECD Development Centre calculations based on Com Trade data.
StatLink: http://dx.doi.org/10.1787/888932606340

Different approaches

It's difficult to give exact numbers for the scale of these aid activities. As we saw in Chapter 3, most of the emerging economies do not report aid figures to the OECD, unlike the traditional donors. And even where data is reported, they don't always use the same definitions for estimating official development assistance (ODA), making precise comparisons between traditional and new donors difficult. So it's necessary to treat any estimates with some caution. Nevertheless, there's a clear sense in recent years that the scale of these efforts is increasing, and that countries such as China, India, Brazil, Saudi Arabia, Turkey and Venezuela are becoming ever more significant aid partners. According to one set of estimates, the new development partners' share of global ODA rose from 1.7% in 1995 to 12% in 2008, and is on track to hit 20%, or one fifth of the global total, in 2015. Other estimates are somewhat lower, but still significant – a recent OECD study estimated non-DAC donors' share of ODA at 8% of the global total in 2009.

But while the scale of these activities is interesting, the way in which emerging economies engage with development partners is perhaps even more striking. It's risky to generalise, but the new donors are often characterised by a different approach to development co-operation, one that emphasises mutual benefits, infrastructure provision, projects rather than general budget support and a lack of conditions on aid.

To look at some of these characteristics in greater detail, the new development partners often emphasise the mutual benefits of working together with a developing country. As we've seen, traditional donors also invoke self-interest for their development activities, but their emphasis tends to be more on longer-term – and perhaps less tangible – benefits, such as improved global security and the creation of new markets. By contrast, the new development partners are more likely to cite immediate returns: development co-operation is often presented as a holistic "win-win" relationship. This is reflected, too, in their approach to funding and investment, which are often bundled together in negotiations along with trade issues.

China has pioneered this approach, but some other BRICS countries (Brazil, Russian Federation, India, China, South Africa) have followed suit: in 2007, for example, Senegal signed a

8. New partners for development

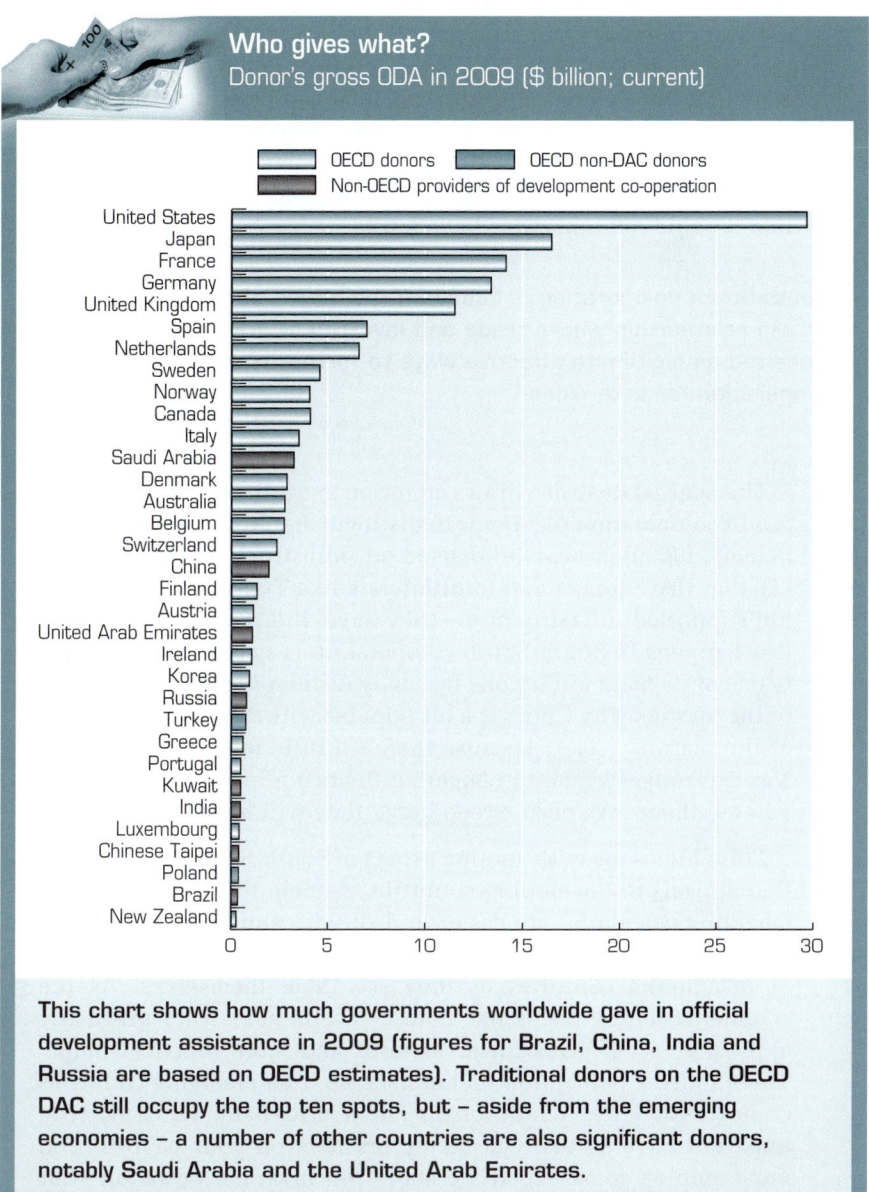

Who gives what?
Donor's gross ODA in 2009 ($ billion; current)

This chart shows how much governments worldwide gave in official development assistance in 2009 (figures for Brazil, China, India and Russia are based on OECD estimates). Traditional donors on the OECD DAC still occupy the top ten spots, but – aside from the emerging economies – a number of other countries are also significant donors, notably Saudi Arabia and the United Arab Emirates.

Source: OECD (2011), "Aggregate Aid Statistics: ODA by donor", *OECD International Development Statistics (database)*, with estimates for Brazil, China, India and Russia as reported by Zimmermann and Smith (2011).
StatLink : http://dx.doi.org/10.1787/888932606359

$2.2 billion deal with India and the steel giant Arcelor Mittal to create an iron-ore extraction project, build a steel plant and a port, and restore and construct railway lines. How much of this deal was economic investment and how much was a classic development initiative? It's hard to say, and, in any case, many would argue, the distinction may not be that important. What may matter more, they would say, is that Senegal got funding for vital infrastructure that it could not otherwise have found.

> "South-South co-operation is based on the notion of a win-win relationship where trade and investment are conceived as legitimate effective ways to further economic co-operation for both sides."
>
> *African Economic Outlook 2011*

The Senegal deal also draws attention to another aspect of South-South co-operation that tends to distinguish it from traditional aid; namely, it's often heavily focused on infrastructure. That's not to say that DAC donors and multilaterals like The World Bank have not supported infrastructure – they have. But the extent to which this happens in South-South co-operation is striking and, indeed, is one of its main attractions for many developing countries. "One of the reasons why China is a bit popular with Africans now – one of the reasons – is … because there's a little more leverage … ," Ngozi Okonjo-Iweala, the Nigerian finance minister, has said. "If you tell them, 'We need a road here,' they will help you build it."

This chimes too with another aspect of South-South co-operation that appeals to developing countries, namely the perception that emerging economies are easier to deal with and less bureaucratic than Western donors, as well as more attuned to the needs of developing countries as they see them themselves. As the economist Jeffrey Sachs has noted, "China has a very pragmatic approach … . It gives fewer lectures and more practical help." There's also a perception that assistance from emerging countries comes with fewer conditions: "The World Bank will say, 'you must not have so many so many teachers on your payroll. You must employ some expatriate staff. You must cut down on your wages,'" Kadi Sesay, a former Sierra Leone government minister, told the academic Deborah Brautigam. "The Chinese will not do this. They will not say, 'You must do this, do that, do this!'."

A further point of appeal is that, unlike many OECD countries, the emerging economies carry no colonial baggage: "The one big advantage China has over its Western rivals is that most African leaders don't perceive it to be a neo-imperial power," the Nigerian academic Adekeye Adebajo has stated.

It's perhaps ironic, then, that one of the main criticisms of the emerging economies, and particularly China, is that they are using development co-operation as a cover for a "neo-imperialist" foreign policy in developing countries, and especially in Africa. "The resource-based corruption and international greed that has typified so much of the West's interactions with African countries has now arrived in the tiny and impoverished West African country of Gabon," writes Khadija Sharife, a journalist and visiting scholar with Centre for Civil Society in South Africa. "Only this time, the external predator, working in tandem with a venal, autocratic local ruler, isn't the West – it's China." Accusations such as this are driven – at least in part – by the characteristics of China's development co-operation policy, which has tended to be strongly driven by foreign policy and economic considerations. (To be fair, such objectives have also played a role in determining the approaches of traditional donors, too, as well as those of other new development partners.) Also, and as with other emerging economies, there isn't always a lot of information available on how much they're spending and what they're spending it on in developing countries, which only tends to fuel speculation. Whether accusations of neo-colonialism are justified overall, however, is a moot point and will, no doubt, continue to be debated.

Other charges are also made against the emerging economies. One is that they turn a blind eye to corruption, in part because they don't tend to impose good governance conditions on developing countries. But governance indicators offer a counterweight to these accusations. For example, the Mo Ibrahim Index, which measures the delivery of public goods and services to citizens, listed Angola and the Democratic Republic of Congo among six African countries with the biggest positive change in their scores in the 2000s; at the same time, both countries concluded huge resource-for-infrastructure deals with China.

One last point is worth noting regarding the new development partners: Much of the aid they provide is tied. This links to a point made earlier, namely that the relationships between countries like

China and India and developing countries are often couched in terms of mutual benefit. In that sense, and from the perspective of the emerging economies, tied aid makes sense; but from the point of view of the developing countries with which they're working, tied aid carries problems, whoever it's from. For one thing, it hampers development of local markets. For another, it raises the cost of goods and services, reducing aid effectiveness. However, in the case of the emerging economies, this may not be quite so much of a problem, as prices for their goods and services are generally lower than those of developed countries.

> "Contrary to widely held beliefs, there is no evidence that the emerging partners have worsened corruption in Africa. In fact, there are signs that it may improve national control over the development agenda in some instances."
>
> *African Economic Outlook 2011*

Thinking triangularly

Despite these criticisms, many people believe the rising involvement of the emerging economies in development co-operation has many positives. They bring a new source of funds and energy, and their own recent experiences of building their own economies give them powerful insights into strategies that can work for other developing countries. Their unique role has been increasingly recognised in the development world. For example, in 2011 the OECD's DAC issued a special statement on the role of the new partners. In it, the traditional donors stated that they "acknowledge the essential role that major nations from beyond our membership have had in contributing to global progress towards the Millennium Development Goals". They said also that they "welcome the contribution of all providers of development co-operation resources and expertise, and hope to forge new relationships with these new partners through open dialogue without preconditions."

How should these relationships proceed? The full answer to that question may take years to emerge, but already there are hints of how things might look. One of the most striking is the idea of **triangular co-operation**, where an established donor works with a new partner (usually referred to as the "pivot country") and a beneficiary developing country. As with much else in

8. New partners for development

development, the idea is less complicated than it might first seem, and an example will help to explain it. Following almost three decades of civil war, Angola in the early 2000s faced the task of trying to rebuild a devastated health system. It requested the assistance of the Japanese government to rebuild the important Josina Machel Hospital. But once the infrastructure was in place, Angola faced a new problem: how to get medical workers to fill it. It turned again to Japan, but the government there felt it lacked the capacity to help train staff. So, the two countries turned to a third "pivot" country, Brazil, which shares the same language as Angola, Portuguese, and is culturally closer. For three years, Japan covered the cost of training and purchased the necessary materials, but the bulk of the training was carried out by Brazilian personnel. In total, more than 700 medical workers were trained.

> "We may have different methods, but our common interest is in reducing global poverty and increasing sustainable and inclusive economic growth."
>
> *OECD DAC Statement: Welcoming New Partnerships in International Development Co-operation*

This sort of three-way co-operation is designed to make best use of countries' "competitive advantage" in development co-operation: in this case, Japan had financial resources and advanced skills in medical technology; Brazil had language and cultural capacities, and experience in delivering healthcare in circumstances that, while not similar to Angola's, was probably closer to it than Japan's. There are other potential benefits, including the possibility of reduced costs: experts and equipment from an emerging economy like Brazil are likely to cost considerably less than if they come from Japan.

The success of projects like this has encouraged rising interest in triangular co-operation. But there have also been some words of warning. For one thing, it's often hard enough to co-ordinate the efforts of two countries; adding a third risks making the task even harder. And, unless projects are carefully worked out, the cost benefits of introducing more experts from developing countries could be lost. There are also concerns about the extent to which the beneficiary developing countries are able to exercise effective control over such initiatives. There's a risk that in the creation of such three-way partnerships, their voices could be lost.

In this, the message for developing countries regarding South-South and triangular co-operation is really no different from the issue of managing their relationships with traditional donors: if they're not in the driving seat and willing – and able – to take full ownership of their own development strategies, the prospects of development success will be greatly diminished.

> "... African policy makers need to ensure that relations with all partners, old and new, are framed to achieve their country's development vision, not their partners'."
> *African Economic Outlook 2011*

By way of conclusion ...

In December 2009, the world of development co-operation marked a small but significant milestone: Korea joined the DAC, the OECD's Development Assistance Committee. Within living memory, a country left devastated and impoverished by conflict had gone from being an aid recipient to a donor. It was a remarkable turnaround. "Half a century ago, Korea was one of the poorest nations in the world, endeavouring to emerge from the ashes of the Korean War to rebuild itself," said Oh Joon, Korea's then-Deputy Minister of Foreign Affairs. From the mid-1940s, for almost five decades, it received $13 billion in aid: "Making good use of this assistance," said Oh Joon, "we worked hard to overcome poverty and achieve development. For many Koreans, including myself, it happened in our own lifetime."

The switch from recipient to donor had a particular resonance for the minister: "As a child, I went to an elementary school where we drank milk and ate corn bread that came in containers marked 'United Nations' or 'US Government'," he recalled. "A few months ago, I visited a kindergarten in Mongolia where children were studying with textbooks marked as gifts from the Republic of Korea."

Korea's story is interesting for many reasons, not the least of which is that – long before the Paris Declaration on Aid Effectiveness – Korea was already essentially implementing many of its principles.

"They really only had two donors, the United States and Japan, so they avoided the harmonisation and transaction costs, and those donors stuck with them through thick and thin, albeit mainly for political reasons," says Brenda Killen, who works on aid effectiveness issues at the OECD. "So Korea had predictability, and alignment. And there were a number of cases where Korea was actually heavily criticised by The World Bank because it did what it wanted to do, especially with protection for infant industries, but you can see that as a sign of strong ownership." Arguably, Korean firms also benefited from a much easier trade regime: things they did back in the early days of their industrialisation might now put them in breach of intellectual property rights. The Doha Development Round was supposed to make trade easier for developing countries, even if it would not have given them the same conditions Korea enjoyed. But Doha is stalled, and many wonder when – or if – an agreement will ever be reached.

Words, action

In late 2011, Korea cemented its changed role in development co-operation by hosting the impressively titled Fourth High-Level Forum on Aid Effectiveness in the port city of Busan. As Korean President Lee Myung-bak reminded delegates, when he was a child this was one of the poorest countries in the world and Busan was used to importing food to stop people starving after the civil war.

It's an event that may not have directly crossed your radar, but in the world of development the Busan meeting was the subject of enormous discussion and great expectations. Much of that focused on how it could help to lay out a new roadmap for a more global partnership for development involving an ever-widening cast of players, including not just the traditional donors and developing countries, but also the likes of China and India, non-governmental organisations (NGOs), major new players like the Gates Foundation, civil society, and so on.

One new departure was the involvement of all these actors in negotiations on what future partnership for development would look like. After extended and often difficult negotiations, 18 sherpas representing governments from all points of the development spectrum, as well as civil society, reached an agreement: the Busan Partnership for Effective Development Co-operation, described as a turning point for international development co-operation – the first "agreed framework for development co-operation that embraces traditional donors, South-South co-operators, the BRICs, CSOs and private funders". They decided to create a new **Global Partnership for Effective Development Co-operation** by June 2012, building on and replacing the existing OECD Working Party on Aid Effectiveness.

> "Never before has there been such an inclusive and fully engaged process behind international development...", the OECD's Secretary-General, Angel Gurría, said, speaking at the final press conference at the event. "While we still have a lot to do, this document... is a roadmap that will take us forward on an agreed path... this is a new agenda. It is not about the sum of the parts. It is not just about 'aid' but about using and strengthening diverse sources of finance, from taxation and domestic resources to aid for trade to private investment to support sustainable and inclusive development".

The OECD itself is also rethinking the whole development relationship in a new strategy for development anchored in partnerships that go beyond aid.

It's easy to be cynical about such words – after all, haven't there been many similar declarations many times before? And wasn't the Doha round supposed to have been agreed years ago? There have and it was. But weighed against such disappointments, it's only fair to acknowledge the achievements. Over the years, there has been much progress and, in some respects, a change of mindset in the way that countries – rich, emerging and poor – work together to overcome poverty. Think of the MDGs, which, even if they may not be met in full, have helped to spur countless initiatives to reduce the impact of poverty. Something similar could be said about the agreements and declarations on aid effectiveness: again, even if they don't have quite the same level of international buy-in, they have helped to change the way development is done. Could more have been done? Undoubtedly yes. At the same time, let's not underestimate just how much has been achieved.

As for the future, one thing is clear. Whatever comes out of the post-Busan process, or any other forum on development co-operation in the years ahead, only one thing is needed to ensure their success: a genuine willingness to work together in our global village to improve the lives of our poorest neighbours. If we can find that, then the prospects of everyone on this planet can only get better.

8. New partners for development

Find Out More

FROM OECD ...

On the Internet

To find out about how the OECD's Development Assistance Committee is **engaging** with emerging economy and other donors, go to *www.oecd.org/dac/opendoors*; to read the Committee's statement on new partnerships in development co-operation, go to *www.oecd.org/dataoecd/7/3/47652500.pdf*

To find out more about **OECD work on the BRICS** countries, go to *www.oecd.org/* and add the relevant country name after the slash – **Brazil, Russia, India, China** and **SouthAfrica** (one word). **Brazil, India** and **South Africa** are also members of the OECD Development Centre. Find out more at *www.oecd.org/dev*

To find out more about the **Busan High-Level Forum**, go to *www.aideffectiveness.org/busanhlf4*

For more about **Angus Maddison**'s groundbreaking research on long-term economic trends, go to *www.theworldeconomy.org*

The **China-DAC Study Group** was formed by the International Poverty Reduction Centre in China (IPRCC) and the DAC in 2009 with the aim of facilitating the sharing of experiences and promoting learning on growth and poverty reduction. Find out more at *www.iprcc.org/publish/page/en/feature/chinadac/2009*

Publications

Perspectives on Global Development (series): From the OECD's Development Centre, this annual series aims to describe and analyse changes in the global economy and the impact of these on the world's developing countries.

African Economic Outlook (series): Produced jointly by the OECD, the African Development Bank and two United Nations agencies, the UN Economic Commission for Africa and the UN Development Programme, this annual reference book brings the latest available economic information for most of the economies of Africa.

The World Economy: A Millennial Perspective (2001), **The World Economy Historical Statistics** (2003) and **Chinese Economic Performance in the Long Run** (1998), by Angus Maddison: An unrivalled long-term perspective on economic trends globally and in China.

... AND OTHER SOURCES

South-South Opportunity (*www.southsouth.info/*) describes itself as a "a community of professionals dedicated to South-South Cooperation, Knowledge Exchange and Learning for development." Visitors to the site may also be interested in the self-explanatory **South-South Opportunity Case Studies** site, which can be accessed at *www.impactalliance.org/ev_en.php?ID=48706_201&ID2=DO_COMMUNITY*.

The **Forum on China-Africa Co-operation** (*www.focac.org/eng*) is an official forum between China and African states; since 2000, four summits have been held under FOCAC's umbrella.

References

Chapter 1

Atwood, B. (2008), "Foreign Assistance Reform: Building US Civilian Development and Diplomatic Capacity in the 21st Century," 25 Jun., Testimony given to the House Committee on Foreign Affairs; *http://pdf.usaid.gov/pdf_docs/PCAAB759.pdf*

Brautigam, D. (2009), *The Dragon's Gift*, Oxford University Press, Oxford and New York.

Darnton, A. (2011), "Aid: why are we still stuck in 1985?" 28 Mar., Poverty Matters Blog, *The Guardian*, Guardian News and Media Ltd., London.

Deutscher, E. (2010), "10 Theses on the future of development co-operation," 16 Dec., Development Assistance Committee, *www.oecd.org/officialdocuments/displaydocumentpdf?cote=dac/chair(2010)7&doclanguage=en*

DFID (2011), "Fair exchange: How UK aid is helping Ethiopian farmers to get the right price for their produce," 29 Jul., Department for International Development, London; *www.dfid.gov.uk/Stories/Case-Studies/2011/Coffee-and-commodities*

Fragomeni, C. (2011), "African famine crisis despair unimaginable," 13 Aug., *The Hamilton Spectator*, Hamilton, Ontario.

Glennie, J. (2011), "The OECD should give up control of the aid agenda," 29 Apr., Poverty Matters Blog, The Guardian, Guardian News and Media Ltd., London.

Hutchison, J. (2010), "Educating Hajra," 7 Jun., Asian Development Bank, Manila, *http://beta.adb.org/news/impact-stories/educating-hajra*

Johnson Sirleaf, E. (2010), "Introduction," in Radelet, S., *Emerging Africa*, Centre for Global Development, Washington.

Moyo, D. (2009), *Dead Aid*, Penguin Books, London.

OECD (2011), "Better Policies for Better Lives – The OECD at 50 and Beyond", OECD, Paris, *www.oecd.org/dataoecd/63/52/47747755.pdf*

OECD (2011), *Development Co-operation Report 2011*, OECD Publishing, *http://dx.doi.org/10.1787/dcr-2010-en*

OECD (2011), *African Economic Outlook 2011: Africa and its Emerging Partners*, OECD Publishing, *http://dx.doi.org/10.1787/aeo-2011-en*

OECD/World Trade Organization (2011), *Aid for Trade at a Glance 2011: Showing Results*, OECD Publishing, *http://dx.doi.org/10.1787/9789264117471-en*

Sachs, J. (2005), *The End of Poverty*, Penguin Books, London.

Chapter 2

Asamoah, Asamoah, C.D. (2010), "One -Third of Accra Residents Live in Slums," 30 Apr., *Public Agenda*, Accra.

Bishop, M. (2009), *Essential Economics – An A-Z Guide*, The Economist/Bloomberg Press, New York.

Collier, P. (2008), *The Bottom Billion*, Oxford University Press, Oxford.

Commission on Growth and Development (2008), *The Growth Report*, The International Bank for Reconstruction and Development/The World Bank, Washington, DC, *http://cgd.s3.amazonaws.com/GrowthReportComplete.pdf*

Guardian, The (2011), "International Day of the Midwife: Voices from Africa," 5 May, *The Guardian*, Guardian News & Media Ltd., London.

Holden, P, M. Bale and S. Holden (2004), *Swimming Against the Tide? An Assessment of the Private Sector in the Pacific*, Asian Development Bank, Manila, Philippines, *www.adb.org/Documents/Books/Swimming_Against_Tide/swimming_against_tide.pdf*

IMF (n.d.), World Economic Outlook Database, International Monetary Fund, *www.imf.org/external/pubs/ft/weo/2010/02/weodata/index.aspx*

References

Keeley, B. (2007), *Human Capital – How What You Know Shapes Your Life*, OECD Insights, OECD Publishing, http://dx.doi.org/10.1787/9789264029095-en

Larson, C. (2010), "Chicago on the Yangtze", *Foreign Policy*, Sept.-Oct.,The Slate Group, Washington DC.

Maddison, A. (2001), *The World Economy: A Millennial Perspective, Development Centre Studies*, OECD Publishing, http://dx.doi.org/10.1787/9789264022621-en

OECD (n.d.), "Glossary of Statistical Terms", http://stats.oecd.org/glossary/index.htm

OECD (2001), *Poverty Reduction: The DAC Guidelines*, OECD Publishing, http://dx.doi.org/0.1787/9789264194779-en

OECD (2006), *Development Co-operation Report 2005*, OECD Publishing, http://dx.doi.org/0.1787/dcr-2005-3-e

OECD (2007), *Promoting Pro-Poor Growth: Policy Guidance for Donors*, OECD Publishing, http://dx.doi.org/10.1787/9789264024786-en

OECD (2010), *Development Co-operation Report 2010*, OECD Publishing, http://dx.doi.org/10.1787/dcr-2010-en

OECD (2010), *Perspectives on Global Development 2010: Shifting Wealth*, OECD Publishing, http://dx.doi.org/10.1787/9789264084728-en

OECD (2011), *Development Co-operation Report 2011*, OECD Publishing, http://dx.doi.org/10.1787/dcr-2011-en

OECD (2012), *Perspectives on Global Development 2012: Social Cohesion in a Shifting World*, OECD Publishing, http://dx.doi.org/10.1787/persp_glob_dev-2012-en

Owen, A.L., J. Videras and L. Davis (2009), "Do all countries follow the same growth process?" *Journal of Economic Growth*, Vol. 14/4, December, Springer.

Radelet, S. (2010), *Emerging Africa: How 17 Countries Are Leading the Way*, Centre for Global Development, Washington.

Summer, A. (2010), "Global Poverty and the New Bottom Billion: What if Three-Quarters of the World's Poor Live in Middle-Income Countries?", Working Paper, 12 Sept., Institute of

Development Studies, London, *www.ids.ac.uk/files/dmfile/ GlobalPovertyDataPaper1.pdf*

United Nations (2011), *The Millennium Development Goals Report 2011*, United Nations Department of Economic and Social Affairs, New York, *www.un.org/millenniumgoals/ reports.shtml*

United Nations Development Programme (2010), *Human Development Report 2010,* Palgrave Macmillan, New York, *http://hdr.undp.org*

United Nations Human Settlements Programme (UN-Habitat) (2010), *Ghana: Accra Urban Profile,* UNON, Publishing Services Section, Nairobi.

Werlin, H. (1991), "Ghana and South Korea: Lessons from World Bank Case Studies," Vol. 11/3, May/Jun., *Public Administration and Development*, Wiley.

Wolfensohn, J. (2007), "The four circles of a changing world", *International Herald Tribune*, 4 Jun., New York Times Co., New York.

World Bank (2012), *World Development Report 2012*, The World Bank, Washington DC, www.worldbank.org

Chapter 3

Barder, O. (2005), "What sort of conditions should there be on aid?," Dec., Owen Abroad blog, *www.owen.org/musings/ conditionality*

BBC News (2010), "Haiti quake witnesses speak of devastation," 13 Jan., British Broadcasting Corp., London.

BBC News (2011), "Report challenges Haiti earthquake death toll," 1 Jun, British Broadcasting Corp., London.

Benn, J., A. Rogerson and S. Steensen (2010), "Getting Closer to the Core – Measuring Country Programmable Aid", June, Issue 1, Development Brief, OECD Development Co-operation Directorate, Paris; *http://oecd.org/dataoecd/32/51/45564447. pdf?contentId=45564448*

References

Bosch, E. (2011), "Making the Most of the International Aid System," *OECD Journal: General Papers,* OECD Publishing, *http://dx.doi.org/10.1787/gen_papers-2010-5kgc6cl35rmr*

Carey, S. (2010), "Moral trade-off muddies aid or trade debate," Jul. 16, *The Irish Times*, The Irish Times Ltd., Dublin.

Degnbol-Martinussen, J. and P. Engberg-Pedersen (2003), *Aid: Understanding International Development Cooperation,* Mellemfolkeligt Samvirke, Copenhagen.

Development Assistance Committee (2003), "Philanthropic Foundations and Development Co-operation," Vol. 4/3, (offprint of the) *DAC Journal,* OECD Publishing, *www.oecd.org/dataoecd/23/4/22272860.pdf*

Jennings, S. (2011) "Time's Bitter Flood," Oxfam GB Research Report, 27 May, Oxfam GB, Oxford, *www.oxfam.org.uk/resources/policy/conflict_disasters/downloads/rr-times-bitter-floods*

Kharas, H., W. Jung and K. Makino (2011), "Overview: An Agenda for the Busan High Level Forum on Aid Effectiveness," in Kharas, H., W. Jung and K. Makino (eds.), *Catalyzing Development A New Vision for Aid*, Brookings Institution Press, Washington DC.

OECD (2004), "Philanthropic Foundations and Development Co-operation", *OECD Journal on Development,* Vol. 4/3, *http://dx.doi.org/10.1787/journal_dev-v4-art23-en*

OECD (2005), *Development Co-operation Report 2005: Efforts and Policies of the Members of the Development Assistance Committee,* OECD Publishing, *http://dx.doi.org/10.1787/dcr-2005-en*

OECD (2007), *Financing Development: Aid and Beyond,* OECD Publishing, *http://dx.doi.org/10.1787/9789264027596-en*

OECD (2008), "Is It ODA?" Factsheet, November, OECD, Paris, *www.oecd.org/dataoecd/21/21/34086975.pdf*

OECD (2009), *Civil Society and Aid Effectiveness: Findings, Recommendations and Good Practice,* OECD Publishing, *http://dx.doi.org/10.1787/9789264056435-en*

OECD (2010), *2008 DAC Report on Multilateral Aid*, OECD Publishing, *http://dx.doi.org/10.1787/9789264097322-en*

OECD (2010), *Development Co-operation Report 2010*, OECD Publishing, *http://dx.doi.org/10.1787/dcr-2010-en*

OECD (2011), *Development Co-operation Report 2011*, OECD Publishing, *http://dx.doi.org/10.1787/20747721*

Radelet, S. (2006), "Working Paper Number 92: A Primer on Foreign Aid," July, Centre for Global Development, Washington DC, *www.cgdev.org/content/publications/detail/8846*

Ramachandran, V. (2010), "India emerges as an aid donor," 5 Oct., *The Huffington Post*.

Riddell, R.C. (2007), *Does Foreign Aid Really Work?* Oxford University Press, Oxford and New York.

Rogerson A. and S. Steensen (2009), "Aid Orphans: Whose Responsibility?" Issue 1, Oct., Development Brief, OECD Development Co-operation Directorate, Paris, *www.oecd.org/dataoecd/14/34/43853485.pdf*

Smith, K. (2011), "Statistical reporting by the Bill & Melinda Gates Foundation to the OECD DAC," April, OECD Development Co-operation Directorate; *www.oecd.org/dataoecd/5/60/47539494.pdf*

State Council Information Office of the People's Republic of China (2011), "China's Foreign Aid", April, SCIO, Beijing; *www.scio.gov.cn/zxbd/wz/201104/t896900.htm*

Tan, E. (2010), "Haiti quake: Aid workers' diaries, Saturday 16 January," 18 Jan., British Broadcasting Corp., London.

United Nations (2009), "The UN in Brief," UN, New York, *www.un.org/Overview/uninbrief*

World Bank (2011), "What We Do", *http://web.worldbank.org*

Worthington, S.A. and T. Pipa (2011), "Private Development Assistance: The Importance of International NGOs and Foundations in a New Aid Architecture," in H. Kharas et al (eds), *Catalyzing Development*, Brookings Institution Press, Washington, DC.

Chapter 4

Adams, J. (2007), "Rising sea levels threaten small Pacific island nations," 3 May, *The New York Times*, The New York Times Co., New York.

Bossuat, G. (2008), "The Marshall Plan: History and Legacy," in Sorel, E. and P.C. Padoan (eds), *The Marshall Plan: Lessons Learned for the 21st Century,* OECD Publishing, *http://dx.doi.org/10.1787/9789264044258-en*

Bulíř, A. and A.-J. Hamann (2008), "Volatility of Development Aid: From the Frying Pan into the Fire?" *World Development*, Vol. 36/10, International Monetary Fund/Elsevier Inc.

Clark, H., "The Real Wealth of Nations: Lessons from the Human Development Report," in OECD (2011), *Development Co-operation Report 2011*, OECD Publishing, *http://dx.doi.org/10.1787/20747721*

CNN (2009), "Obama: Troops Alone Cannot Win in Afghanistan," 19 Feb, *www.cnn.com*

Dabla-Norris, E., C. Minoiu and L.-F. Zanna (2010), "Business Cycle Fluctuations, Large Shocks, and Development Aid: New Evidence," IMF Working Paper, WP/10/240, International Monetary Fund, Washington, DC, *www.imf.org/external/pubs/ft/wp/2010/wp10240.pdf*

Degnbol-Martinussen, J. and P. Engberg-Pedersen (2003), *Aid: Understanding International Development Cooperation*, Mellemfolkeligt Samvirke, Copenhagen.

Derviş, K., H. Kharas and N. Unger (2010), *Aiding Assistance Reform for the 21st Century: Brookings Blum Roundtable 2010*, Brookings, Washington DC, *www.brookings.edu/events/2010/0804_development.aspx*

G20 (2010), "Seoul Development Consensus for Shared Growth," The G20 Seoul Summit Leaders' Declaration, Annex 1, Nov. 11–12, Seoul, *www.g20.org/Documents2010/11/seoulsummit_annexes.pdf*

Hjertholm, P. and H. White (2000), "Foreign Aid in Historical Perspective," in F. Tarp (ed), *Foreign Aid and Development*, Routledge, London and New York.

Irish Aid (2010), "Bringing parliament to the people," last updated 22 Dec., Department of Foreign Affairs, Dublin: accessed at *www.irishaid.gov.ie/article.asp?article=1732*

Kagame, P. (2009), "Africa has to find its own road to prosperity," 7 May, *Financial Times*, The Financial Times Ltd., London.

Moyo, D. (2009), *Dead Aid*, Penguin Books, London.

Morella, C.A. (2008), "Marshall Plan 60th Anniversary Symposium: Introductory Remarks", in Sorel, E. and P.C. Padoan (eds) (2008), *The Marshall Plan: Lessons Learned for the 21st Century*, OECD Publishing, *http://dx.doi.org/10.1787/9789264044258-en*

National Research Council, The (1978), *The U.S. Government Foreign Disaster Assistance Program*, National Academy of Sciences, Washington, DC, *http://pdf.usaid.gov/pdf_docs/PNADQ468.pdf*

Obama, B. (2010), "Remarks by the President at the Millennium Development Goals Summit in New York, New York", 22 Sep., United Nations Headquarters, New York, NY, *www.whitehouse.gov/the-press-office/2010/09/22/remarks-president-millennium*

OECD (2005), *Development Co-operation Report 2004*, OECD Publishing, *http://dx.doi.org/10.1787/dcr-2004-en*

OECD (2006), United States – Development Assistance Committee (DAC) Peer Review, OECD, Paris, *www.oecd.org/dataoecd/61/57/37885999.pdf*

OECD (2008), France – Development Assistance Committee (DAC) Peer Review, OECD, Paris; *www.oecd.org/dataoecd/4/10/40814790.pdf*

OECD (2009), *Integrating Climate Change Adaptation into Development Co-operation: Policy Guidance*, OECD Publishing, *http://dx.doi.org/10.1787/9789264054950-en*

OECD (2009), *Development Co-operation Report 2009*, OECD Publishing, *http://dx.doi.org/10.1787/dcr-2009-en*

OECD (2010), *Development Co-operation Report 2010*, OECD Publishing, *http://dx.doi.org/10.1787/dcr-2010-en*

OECD (2011), *Development Co-operation Report 2011*, OECD Publishing, *http://dx.doi.org/10.1787/20747721*

Opeskin, B.R. (1996), "The Moral Foundations of Foreign Aid," in Vol. 24/1, *World Development*, Elsevier Science Ltd.

Radelet, S. (2006), "Working Paper Number 92: A Primer on Foreign Aid," July, Centre for Global Development, Washington DC, *www.cgdev.org/content/publications/detail/8846*

Riddell, R.C. (2007), *Does Foreign Aid Really Work?* Oxford University Press, Oxford and New York.

Rogerson A. and S. Steensen (2009), "Aid Orphans: Whose Responsibility?" Issue 1, Oct., Development Brief, OECD Development Co-operation Directorate, Paris; accessed at *www.oecd.org/dataoecd/14/34/43853485.pdf*

Sachs, J. (2005), *The End of Poverty: Economic Possibilities for Our Time*, The Penguin Press, New York.

Truman, H.S. (1949), "Truman's Inaugural Address," 20 Jan., Harry S. Truman Library and Museum, *www.trumanlibrary.org*

World Bank (1990), *World Development Report 1990*, Oxford University Press, Oxford and New York.

World Bank (2010), *World Development Report 2010*, The World Bank, Washington, DC.

Chapter 5

Agence France-Presse (2011), "Malaria on way out in third of nations hit: study," 17 Oct., AFP, Paris, *www.france24.com*

Banerjee, A. and E. Duflo (2011), "More Than 1 Billion People Are Hungry in the World," May/Jun., *Foreign Policy*, The Slate Group, Washington DC.

Barder, O. (2006), "A Policymakers' Guide to Dutch Disease," Working Paper No. 91, Jul., Centre for Global Development, Washington, DC.

Bennett, J. et al (2010), *Aiding the Peace: A Multi-donor Evaluation of Support to Conflict Prevention and Peacebuilding Activities in Southern Sudan 2005-2010*, ITAD Ltd., United Kingdom, *www.oecd.org/dataoecd/3/40/46895095.pdf*

Centre for Global Development (n.d.), "Controlling Tuberculosis in China," Centre for Global Development, Washington, DC, *www.cgdev.org/doc/millions/MS_case_3.pdf*

Chan, M. and R. Chambers (2010), "Defeating malaria is within our grasp," 14 Dec., Poverty Matters Blog, *The Guardian*, Guardian News and Media Ltd., London.

Clements, P., T. Chianca and R. Sasaki (2008), "Reducing World Poverty by Improving Evaluation of Development Aid," *American Journal of Evaluation*, Vol. 29/2, Sage Publications/ American Evaluation Association.

Collier, P. (2008), *The Bottom Billion*, Oxford University Press, Oxford.

DFID (2011), "Battling malaria in India," 19 Apr., Department for International Development, London, *www.dfid.gov.uk/Media-Room/Case-Studies*

Eurobarometer (2007), "Citizens of the new EU Member States and Development Aid," Special Eurobarometer 286, European Commission, Brussels, *http://ec.europa.eu/public_opinion/archives/ebs/ebs_286_en.pdf*

Eurobarometer (2010), "Development Aid in Times of Economic Turmoil," Special Eurobarometer 318, European Commission, Brussels, *http://ec.europa.eu/development/icenter/repository/eurobarometer200910_en.pdf*

Fransman, J. and H.-B. Solignac Lecomte (2004), "Mobilising Public Opinion Against Global Poverty," Apr., No. 2, Policy Insights, OECD Development Centre, Paris, *www.oecd.org/dataoecd/33/41/31484642.pdf*

References

Freschi, L. (2010), "Americans appalled at how much we spend on aid, want to spend 10 times more," 6 Dec., AidWatch blog, Development Research Institute at New York University, New York, *http://aidwatchers.com*

Glennie, J. (2008), *The Trouble With Aid*, Zed Books, London and New York.

Gourevitch, P. (2010), "Alms Dealers," 11 Oct., *The New Yorker*, Condé Nast, New York.

Gurría, A. (2008), "The Global Dodgers," 27 Nov., *The Guardian*, Guardian News and Media Ltd., London.

Hotez, P.J. (2009), "How to Cure 1 Billion People? Defeat Neglected Tropical Diseases," Dec. 21, *Scientific American*, Scientific American, Inc., New York

International Bank for Reconstruction and Development/World Bank (1998), *Assessing Aid*, Oxford University Press, Inc., New York.

Kelland, K. (2011), "Malaria kills more than 780,000 people a year worldwide," 17 Oct., Reuters, London, *www.reuters.com*

Kremer, M. and E. Miguel (2011), "Primary School Deworming In Kenya," Abdul Latif Jameel Poverty Action, Massachusetts Institute of Technology, Cambridge, MA, *www.povertyactionlab.org/evaluation/primary-school-deworming-kenya*

McGillivray, M. (n.d.) "Is Aid Effective?" (Draft) WIDER, Helsinki, Finland, *www.oecd.org/dataoecd/18/39/34353462.pdf*

Mwenda, A.M. (2008) "Aid creates the wrong incentives for progress", 24 Jul., *The Guardian*, Guardian News and Media Ltd., London, *http://www.guardian.co.uk/katine/2008/jul/23/africaaid.background1*

Natsios, A. (2010), "The Dangers of Development Metrics," 20 Dec., GMF Blog, German Marshall Fund of the United States, *http://blog.gmfus.org/2010/12/the-dangers-of-development-metrics*

OECD (1986), *Development Co-operation Report 1985*, OECD Publishing.

OECD (2002), *Glossary of Key Terms in Evaluation and Results Based Management*, OECD Publishing, http://dx.doi.org/10.1787/9789264034921-en-fr

OECD (2003), "Philanthropic Foundations and Development Co-operation," *DAC Journal*, Vol. 4/3, OECD Publishing.

OECD (2010), *Evaluation in Development Agencies*, OECD Publishing, http://dx.doi.org/10.1787/9789264094857-en

OECD DAC Network on Development Evaluation (2010), *Evaluation Development Co-operation – Summary of Key Norms and Standards*, June, 2nd ed., OECD, Paris, www.oecd.org/dac/evaluation

Radelet, S. (2006), "A Primer on Foreign Aid," Working Paper No. 92, Jul., Centre for Global Development, Washington DC, www.cgdev.org/content/publications/detail/8846

Riddell, R.C. (2007), *Does Foreign Aid Really Work?* Oxford University Press, Oxford and New York.

Schaefer, B.D. (2010) "Development in Africa is Not About Aid," Spring, *The Forum*, Center for International Relations, Arlington, VA.

Svensson, J. (2006), "The Institutional Economics of Foreign Aid," Vol. 13, *Swedish Economic Policy Review*, Swedish Economic Policy Review, Economic Council of Sweden, Stockholm.

Tupy, M.L. (2011), "Foreign Aid Isn't the Answer," 31 Mar., *The Wall Street Journal Europe*, Dow Jones & Co., Inc., New York.

UNESCO-UIS (2011), *Financing Education in sub-Saharan Africa: Meeting the Challenges of Expansion, Equity and Quality*, UNESCO Institute for Statistics, Montreal, www.uis.unesco.org/template/pdf/EducGeneral/Finance_EN_web.pdf

WHO (2010), *World Malaria Report 2010*, World Health Organization, Geneva, www.who.int/malaria

Chapter 6

Ambraseys, N. and R. Bilham (2011), "Corruption kills", 13 Jan., Vol. 469, *Nature*, Nature Publishing Group.

Asian Development Bank/OECD/Transparency International (2007), *Curbing Corruption in Tsunami Relief Operations*, Asian Development Bank, Manila, http://dx.doi.org/10.1787/9789264041387-en

Barder, O. (2011), "Show, Don't Tell," Issue 18, *Public Service Review: International Development,* Publicservice.co.uk Ltd., Newcastle-under-Lyme.

Cairns Group (n.d.), "Domestic Support: Impacting negatively on developing countries' agricultural export interests," The Cairns Group, http://cairnsgroup.org/DocumentLibrary/domestic_support.pdf

Campion, M. J. (2011), "Bribery in India: A website for whistleblowers," 5 Jun., BBC News, British Broadcasting Corp., London, www.bbc.co.uk/news/world-south-asia-13616123

Celasun, O. and J. Walliser (2008), "Managing Aid Surprises," Sept., Vol. 45/3, *Finance & Development,* International Monetary Fund, Washington, DC, http://www.imf.org/external/pubs/ft/fandd/2008/09/celasun.htm

Chissano, J.A. (2007), "Why We Should 'Rethink' Aid," 11-12 Jun., address at New Directions in Development Assistance conference, Rhodes House, Oxford, http://www.clubofmozambique.com/solutions1/investor/docs/ChissanoSpeech.pdf

Collier, P. (2008), *The Bottom Billion*, Oxford University Press, Oxford.

Djankova, S., J.G. Montalvoc, and M. Reynal-Querolc (2009), "Aid with Multiple Personalities," *Journal of Comparative Economics*, Vol. 37/ 2, Jun., Elsevier.

Frot, E. and J. Santiso (2010), "Crushed Aid: Fragmentation in Sectoral Aid," OECD Development Centre Working Paper No. 284, OECD, Paris, http://dx.doi.org/10.1787/218465127786

Kaufmann, D. (2009), "Aid Effectiveness and Governance," Feb., *Development Outreach*, World Bank Institute, Washington, DC.

Kharas, H., W. Jung and K. Makino (2011), "Overview: An Agenda for the Busan High Level Forum on Aid Effectives," in Kharas, H., W. Jung and K. Makino (eds.), *Catalyzing Development A New Vision for Aid*, Brookings Institution Press, Washington DC.

Killen, B. (2010), "The Paris Declaration: Five reasons Why it is Working," *OECD Journal: General Papers*, Vol. 2010/1, OECD Publishing, *http://dx.doi.org/10.1787/gen_papers-2010-5kgc6cl3qfjb*

Kramer, W. M. (2007), "Corruption and Fraud in International Aid Projects," May, No. 4, U4 Brief, U4-Chr. Michelsen Institute, Bergen, *www.U4.no*

Love, P. and P. Lattimore (2009), *International Trade – Free, Fair and Open?*, OECD Insights, OECD Publishing, *http://dx.doi.org/10.1787/9789264055780-en*

Mold, A. (2009), *Policy Ownership and Aid Conditionality in the Light of the Financial Crisis*, OECD Publishing, *http://dx.doi.org/10.1787/9789264075528-en*

Ndikumana, L. (2010) "Challenges for International Development Aid to Africa: Interview, Prof. Léonce Ndikumana," Spring, *The Forum*, Center for International Relations, Arlington, VA.

Nolen, S. (2004), "Africa Battles to Keep Doctors, Nurses," 28 Sept., *The Globe and Mail*, Toronto.

OECD DAC Network on Governance – Anti-Corruption Task Team (n.d.), *Working Towards More Effective Collective Donor Responses To Corruption*, OECD, Paris, *www.oecd.org/dataoecd/26/52/45019669.pdf*

OECD (2006), *Development Co-operation Report 2005*, OECD Publishing, *http://dx.doi.org/10.1787/dcr-2005-en*

OECD (2008), *Financing Development 2008: Whose Ownership?*, Development Centre Studies, OECD Publishing, *http://dx.doi.org/10.1787/9789264045590-en*

References

OECD (2008), *The Paris Declaration on Aid Effectiveness and the Accra Agenda for Action,* OECD, Paris, www.oecd.org/dataoecd/11/41/34428351.pdf

OECD (2009), *2009 OECD Report on Division of Labour,* OECD, Paris, www.oecd.org/dataoecd/18/52/44318319.pdf

OECD (2010), "Trading out of Poverty: How Aid for Trade can Help," *OECD Journal on Development,* OECD Publishing, Vol. 10/2, http://dx.doi.org/10.1787/journal_dev-v10-art16-en

OECD (2010), *Development Co-operation Report 2010,* OECD Publishing, http://dx.doi.org/10.1787/dcr-2010-en

OECD (2011), *Trade for Growth and Poverty Reduction,* OECD Publishing, http://dx.doi.org/10.1787/9789264098978-en

OECD (2011), *Better Policies for Development – Recommendations for Policy Coherence 2011,* OECD, Paris, www.oecd.org/dataoecd/6/57/48110465.pdf

OECD/World Trade Organization (n.d.), "Aid for Trade: Is it Working?" OECD, Paris, www.oecd.org/dataoecd/30/36/45581702.pdf

OECD/World Trade Organization (2011), *Aid for Trade at a Glance 2011: Showing Results,* OECD Publishing, http://dx.doi.org/10.1787/9789264117471-en

OECDEvalNet (2011), "Paris Declaration Evaluation: Malawi Country Report," video interview with Mr. Twaib Ali, uploaded 12 Aug., www.youtube.com/watch?v=MzXAnCbUxPs

Pfutze, T. (2010), "The Importance of Aid Fragmentation in Sub-Saharan Africa," Spring, *The Forum,* Centre for International Relations, Arlington, VA.

Renzio, de, P., L. Whitfield and I. Bergamaschi (2008), "Reforming Foreign Aid Practices," Jun., Global Economic Governance Programme Briefing Paper, Deptartment of Politics and International Relations, University College, Oxford.

Riddell, R.C. (2007), *Does Foreign Aid Really Work?* Oxford University Press, Oxford and New York.

Tavares, J. (2003), "Does foreign aid corrupt?", *Economics Letters,* Vol. 79, Elsevier Science B.V.

Thornton, N., A. Barrington and K. Carroll (2010), "Joint Evaluation of the Paris Declaration – Phase 2 Donor HQ Study – Irish Aid," Agulhas, London, *www.oecd.org/ dataoecd/61/51/47083236.pdf*

Transparency International (2006), "Corruption in Humanitarian Aid," Working Paper No. 3, Transparency International, Berlin.

Transparency International (2007), "Poverty, Aid and Corruption," Policy Paper No. 1/2007, Transparency International, Berlin.

Walker, P. (2007), "Opportunities for Corruption in a Celebrity Disaster," in Asian Development Bank, OECD/Transparency International, *Curbing Corruption in Tsunami Relief Operations,* Asian Development Bank, Manila; *http://dx.doi.org/10.1787/9789264041387-en*

Whitfield, L. (ed) (2009), *The Politics of Aid,* Oxford University Press, Oxford and New York.

Wood, B. et al (2011), *The Evaluation of the Paris Declaration: Final Report,* Danish Institute for International Studies, Copenhagen; accessed at *www.oecd.org/dataoecd/ 5/37/48113803.pdf*

Chapter 7

Bahadur, J. (2010), "Pirates Inc.", 23 Jun., *Financial Times,* The Financial Times Ltd., London.

Brautigam, D. et al (eds) (2008), *Taxation and State-Building in Developing Countries – Capacity and Consent,* Cambridge University Press, Cambridge.

Carter, A. and A. Cebreiro (2011), "Africa's tax system: A survey," No. 284, Q1 2011, *OECD Observer,* OECD Paris, *www.oecdobserver.org/news/categoryfront.php/id/60/Taxation.html*

DFID (2010), "Market women secure a decent trade in Ghana," 21 Sept., Department for International Development, London, *www.dfid.gov.uk/Media-Room/Case-Studies*

References

DFID (2011), "Government to suspend general budget support to Malawi," 14 Jul., Department for International Development, London, *www.dfid.gov.uk/News*

Global Financial Integrity (2010), "Illicit Financial Flows from Africa: Hidden Resource for Development," March, Global Financial Integrity-Centre for International Policy, Washington, DC.

G20 (2009), "London Summit – Leaders' Statement," 2 Apr., London, G20, *www.g20.org/Documents/g20_communique_020409.pdf*

Hyden, G. et al (2004), *Making Sense of Governance: Empirical Evidence from 16 Developing Countries,* Overseas Development Institute, London.

James, J. (2010), "Will Ivorian party spirit end the coups?," 28 Oct., BBC News, British Broadcasting Corp., London.

Keeley, B. (2011), "Conflict – the enemy of development," 11 Apr., OECD Insights Blog, OECD, Paris, *http://oecdinsights.org/2011/04/11/conflict---the-enemy-of-development*

OECD (1995), "Participatory Development and Good Governance", Development Co-operation Guidelines Series, OECD, Paris, *www.oecd.org/dataoecd/27/13/31857685.pdf*

OECD (2006), *Integrating Human Rights and Development,* OECD Publishing, *http://dx.doi.org/10.1787/9789264022102-en*

OECD (2007), "DAC Action-oriented Paper on Human Rights and Development", OECD, Paris, *www.oecd.org/dataoecd/50/7/39350774.pdf*

OECD (2008), *Governance, Taxation and Accountability: Issues and Practices,* OECD, Paris, *www.oecd.org/dataoecd/52/35/40210055.pdf*

OECD (2010), *Citizen-State Relations: Improving Governance Through Tax Reform,* OECD, Paris, *www.oecd.org/dataoecd/19/60/46008596.pdf*

OECD (2010), "Investing in Women and Girls," based on a speech by Jon Lomøy at the Helsinki High-level Symposium, UN 2010 Development Co-operation Forum, 4 June, OECD, Paris, *www.oecd.org/dataoecd/45/55/45704694.pdf*

OECD (2010), *Atlas of Gender and Development: How Social Norms Affect Gender Equality in Non-OECD Countries,* OECD Publishing, *http://dx.doi.org/10.1787/9789264077478-en*

OECD (2010), "DAC Special Review of Poland," OECD, Paris, *www.oecd.org/dataoecd/58/43/45362587.pdf*

OECD (2011), "OECD's Current Tax Agenda", April, OECD, Paris, *www.oecd.org/dataoecd/38/17/1909369.pdf*

OECD (2011), *Supporting Statebuilding in Situations of Conflict and Fragility,* OECD Publishing, *http://dx.doi.org/10.1787/9789264074989-en*

OECD/African Development Bank/United Nations Economic Commission for Africa (2010), *African Economic Outlook 2010,* OECD Publishing, *http://dx.doi.org/10.1787/aeo-2010-en*

Owens, J. (2010), "Tax for Development," Dec. 2009-Jan. 2010, No. 276-277, *OECD Observer,* OECD, Paris, *www.oecdobserver.org/news/fullstory.php/aid/3134/Tax_for_development.html*

Owens, J. and R. Parry (2009), "Why tax matters for development," Jun., No. 273, *OECD Observer,* OECD, Paris, *www.oecdobserver.org/news/fullstory.php/aid/2943*

Roosevelt, F.D. (1936), "Address at Worcester, Mass," Oct. 21, The American Presidency Project, *www.presidency.ucsb.edu*

Sida (2011), "I voted for the first time in my life," 21 Oct., Swedish International Development Cooperation Agency, Stockholm, *www.sida.se*

Solignac Lecomte, H.-B. (2010), "Taxation for Development in Africa: A Shared Responsibility," Jul.-Aug., Vol. 9/6, *Trade Negotiations Insights,* The International Centre for Trade and Sustainable Development, Geneva.

Soto, de, H. (2011), "The Amazon is not Avatar," in *Development Co-operation Report 2011,* OECD Publishing, *http://dx.doi.org/10.1787/20747721*

UNDP (2011), "Illicit Financial Flows from the Least Developed Countries: 1990-2008," May, Discussion Paper, United Nations Development Programme, New York, *www.undp.org/governance*

World Bank, The (2011), *The World Development Report 2011 – Conflict, Security, and Development*, The World Bank, Washington, DC, *http://wdr2011.worldbank.org*

Chapter 8

Alden, C. (2007), *China in Africa*, Zed Books, London and New York.

BBC News (2009), "China praised for African links," 11 Oct., British Broadcasting Corp., London, *http://news.bbc.co.uk/2/hi/8301826.stm*

Brautigam, D. (2009), *The Dragon's Gift*, Oxford University Press, Oxford and New York.

China-DAC Study Group (2009), "Development Partnerships for Growth and Poverty Reduction," 28-29 Oct., Beijing, OECD/International Poverty Reduction Centre in China, *www.oecd.org/dataoecd/11/3/47715065.pdf*

Fordelone, T.Y. (2009), "Triangular Co-operation and Aid Effectiveness – Can Triangular Co-operation Make Aid More Effective?", paper prepared for the Policy Dialogue on Development Co-operation, Mexico City, 28-29 Sept., OECD, Paris, *www.oecd.org/dataoecd/63/37/46387212.pdf*

Francis, N. and M. Francis (2011), "China's meeting with Africa," 30 Jun., *The Guardian*, Guardian News and Media, Ltd., London.

French, H.W. (2010), "The Next Empire," *The Atlantic*, The Atlantic Monthly Group, Washington, DC.

Gurría, A. (2010), "Perspectives on Global Development: Shifting Wealth," remarks for the launch of Perspectives on Global Development 2010, 16 Jun., OECD, Paris, *www.oecd.org/document/6/0,3746,en_2649_33959_45484486_1_1_1_1,00.html*

Halligan, L. (2011), "The BRIC countries' Hainan summit could make the G20 redundant," 16 Apr., *The Telegraph*, Telegraph Media Group Ltd., London.

Maddison, A. (1994), "Confessions of a Chiffrephile," (first published in *Banca Nazionale del Lavoro Quarterly Review*, No. 189, Jun.) Groningen Growth and Development Centre,

University of Groningen, *www.ggdc.net/maddison/Personal/ Autobiog1994.pdf*

OECD (n.d.), "OECD Development Assistance Committee (DAC) Welcomes Korean Membership," press release, OECD, Paris, *www.oecd.org/document/50/0,3343, en_2649_33721_44141618_1_1_1_1,00.html*

OECD (1986), *Development Co-operation Report 1985,* OECD Publishing.

OECD (2010), *Perspectives on Global Development 2010: Shifting Wealth,* OECD Publishing, *http://dx.doi. org/10.1787/9789264084728-en*

OECD (2011), *African Economic Outlook 2011: Africa and its Emerging Partners,* OECD Publishing, *http://dx.doi. org/10.1787/aeo-2011-en*

OECD (2012), *Perspectives on Global Development 2012: Social Cohesion in a Shifting World,* OECD Publishing, *http://dx.doi. org/10.1787/persp_glob_dev-2012-en*

Okonjo-Iweala, N. (2007), "Ngozi Okonjo-Iweala on aid versus trade," June, TED Global 2007, *www.ted.com/talks*

Park, K. (2011), "New Development Partners and a Global Development Partnership," in Kharas, H., W. Jung and K. Makino (eds.), *Catalyzing Development A New Vision for Aid,* Brookings Institution Press, Washington DC.

Rampell, C. (2010), "Angus Maddison, Economic Historian, Dies at 83," 1 May, *The New York Times,* The New York Times Co., New York.

Rice, X. (2011), "China's economic invasion of Africa," 6 Feb., *The Guardian,* Guardian News and Media, Ltd., London.

Sachs, J (2007), "China's lessons for the World Bank," 24 May, *The Guardian,* Guardian News and Media, Ltd., London.

Santiso, J. (2007), "China: A Helping Hand for Latin America?" in *The Visible Hand of China in Latin America,* OECD Publishing, *http://dx.doi.org/10.1787/9789264028388-3-en*

Sharife, K. (2009), "China's New Colonialism," 25 Sept., *Foreign Policy,* The Slate Group, Washington DC.

References

Task Team on South-South Co-operation (n.d.), "Brazil-Angola-Japan – Building Capacities at the Josina Machel Hospital," The South-South Opportunity Case Stories, *www.southsouthcases.info*

UNDP (2009), *Enhancing South-South and Triangular Co-operation,* United Nations Development Programme, New York, *http://southsouthconference.org/wp-content/uploads/2009/10/E_Book.pdf*

Zhang, W.W. (2006), "The allure of the Chinese model," 1 Nov., *International Herald Tribune,* The New York Times Co., New York.

Zimmerman, F. and K. Smith (2011), "More Actors, More Money, More Ideas for International Development Co-operation", in *Journal of International Development,* John Wiley & Sons, Ltd.

Photos credits:

Cover illustration: © TebNad/Fotolia.com.
Images: pp. 8-9: © Birute Vijeikiene/Dreamstime.com
pp. 22-23 © Samrat35/Dreamstime.com
pp. 46-47 © Concetta Zingale/Dreamstime.com
pp. 66-67 © David Snyder/Dreamstime.com
pp. 84-85 © Dmitry Knorre/Dreamstime.com
pp. 102-103 © Jarenwicklund/Dreamstime.com
pp. 124-125 © Smandy/Dreamstime.com
pp. 146-147 © Project1photography/Dreamstime.com.

ORGANISATION FOR ECONOMIC CO-OPERATION AND DEVELOPMENT

The OECD is a unique forum where governments work together to address the economic, social and environmental challenges of globalisation. The OECD is also at the forefront of efforts to understand and to help governments respond to new developments and concerns, such as corporate governance, the information economy and the challenges of an ageing population. The Organisation provides a setting where governments can compare policy experiences, seek answers to common problems, identify good practice and work to co-ordinate domestic and international policies.

The OECD member countries are: Australia, Austria, Belgium, Canada, Chile, the Czech Republic, Denmark, Estonia, Finland, France, Germany, Greece, Hungary, Iceland, Ireland, Israel, Italy, Japan, Korea, Luxembourg, Mexico, the Netherlands, New Zealand, Norway, Poland, Portugal, the Slovak Republic, Slovenia, Spain, Sweden, Switzerland, Turkey, the United Kingdom and the United States. The European Union takes part in the work of the OECD.

OECD Publishing disseminates widely the results of the Organisation's statistics gathering and research on economic, social and environmental issues, as well as the conventions, guidelines and standards agreed by its members.

OECD PUBLISHING, 2, rue André-Pascal, 75775 PARIS CEDEX 16
(012011101P) ISBN 978-92-64-11152-3 – No. 60077 2012